The Road to Hillsborough

The Shaping of the Anglo-Irish Agreement

CW00384760

The Road to Hillsborough

The Shaping of the Anglo-Irish Agreement

by
ANTHONY KENNY
Master of Balliol College, Oxford

PERGAMON PRESS
OXFORD · NEW YORK · BEIJING · FRANKFURT
SÃO PAULO · SYDNEY · TOKYO · TORONTO

U.K.	Pergamon Press, Headington Hill Hall, Oxford OX3 0BW, England
U.S.A.	Pergamon Press, Maxwell House, Fairview Park, Elmsford, New York 10523, U.S.A.
PEOPLE'S REPUBLIC OF CHINA	Pergamon Press, Qianmen Hotel, Beijing, People's Republic of China
FEDERAL REPUBLIC OF GERMANY	Pergamon Press, Hammerweg 6, D-6242 Kronberg, Federal Republic of Germany
BRAZIL	Pergamon Editora, Rua Eça de Queiros, 346, CEP 04011, São Paulo, Brazil
AUSTRALIA	Pergamon Press Australia, P.O. Box 544, Potts Point, N.S.W. 2011, Australia
JAPAN	Pergamon Press, 8th Floor, Matsuoka Central Building, 1-7-1 Nishishinjuku, Shinjuku-ku, Tokyo 160, Japan
CANADA	Pergamon Press Canada, Suite 104, 150 Consumers Road, Willowdale, Ontario M2J 1P9, Canada

Copyright © 1986 Anthony Kenny

All Rights Reserved. No part of this publication may be reproduced, stored in a retrieval system or transmitted in any form or by any means: electronic, electrostatic, magnetic tape, mechanical, photocopying, recording or otherwise, without permission in writing from the publishers.

First edition 1986

Library of Congress Cataloging in Publication Data

Kenny, Anthony John Patrick.
The road to Hillsborough.
Bibliography: p.
1. Northern Ireland—Politics and government—
1969–   . 2. Great Britain. Treaties, etc.
Ireland, 1985 Nov. 15.   I. Title.
DA990.U46K465   1987   941.6082'4   86–42955

British Library Cataloguing in Publication Data

Kenny, Anthony
The road to Hillsborough.
1. Northern Ireland—Politics and government
I. Title
941.608   DA990.U46
ISBN 0-08-034775-4 Hardcover
ISBN 0-08-034248-5 Flexicover

Printed in Great Britain by A. Wheaton & Co. Ltd., Exeter

Preface

On 15 November 1985, the day on which the Prime Ministers of the United Kingdom and of the Republic of Ireland signed an agreement at Hillsborough Castle, I happened to be in Belfast, addressing a seminar of senior civil servants. As news of the agreement reached us, Catholics and Protestants looked at each other significantly. We discussed the implications of the accord, and made conjectures about its prospects. 'We know one thing', someone remarked. 'The date of 15 November will go down in the calendar of Northern Ireland. But whether it will go down for good or ill, who can say?'

This book is an attempt to explain, to English readers, why 15 November 1985 is such a significant day in the history of the province. It seeks to set it in its historical context and also to examine its political implications. In particular, it examines the constitutional proposals and initiatives which preceded it, and explains why the majority of those most closely affected by it regarded it as an insult and an outrage.

During the months after the signing of the Accord, we have not yet seen justified either the fears of those who regarded it as a recipe for civil war, nor the hopes of those who expected it to inaugurate an era of peace, reconciliation and stability. We must wait a long while yet before we can make a balanced judgement on the merits and demerits of Hillsborough.

This is not a scholarly work of history: it is an interim attempt to make recent events in Northern Ireland comprehensible to some readers on mainland Britain. Because of this, I have not burdened the text with an apparatus of footnotes. But it would be churlish not to acknowledge the work of those on whom I have drawn, and therefore I have attached a Note on Sources which will reveal my indebtedness.

Balliol, July 1986   ANTHONY KENNY

Contents

Abbreviations

DUP	Democratic Unionist Party
FF	Fianna Fail
FG	Fine Gael
GAA	Gaelic Athletic Association
INLA	Irish National Liberation Army
IPP	Irish Parliamentary Party
IRA	Irish Republican Army
OUP	Official Unionist Party
PD	People's Democracy
PD	Progressive Democrats
PIRA	Provisional Irish Republican Army
PR	Proportional Representation
PSF	Provisional Sinn Fein
RIC	Royal Irish Constabulary
RUC	Royal Ulster Constabulary
SDLP	Social Democratic and Labour Party
SF	Sinn Fein
UDA	Ulster Defence Association
UDR	Ulster Defence Regiment
UPRG	Ulster Political Research Group
USC	Ulster Special Constabulary
UUUC	United Ulster Unionist Council
UVY	Ulster Volunteer Force
UWC	Ulster Workers Council

A Note on Sources

I found Robert Kee's *The Green Flag* (Quartet Books, 1976) one of the most fair and lively general histories of Ireland up to 1923; his *Ireland, A History* (Abacus, 1982) abbreviates the story and brings it up to date. Patrick Buckland's *A History of Northern Ireland* (Gill and Macmillan, 1981) offers a political survey of the province from its foundation in the early 1920s to the outbreak of violence in the 1970s. A classic Nationalist account of the history of Ireland in the early part of the present century is *The Irish Republic* by Dorothy Macardle (Irish Press, 1951). A Unionist perspective on the history of Northern Ireland is given by A. T. Q. Stewart, *The Narrow Ground: Aspects of Ulster, 1609–1969.*

An excellent account of the stance of the various political groupings immediately before the New Ireland Forum is Padraig O'Malley's book *The Uncivil Wars.* A series of papers by many hands, analysing the political situation in Northern Ireland and comparing it with other areas facing similar problems, is *Political Co-operation in Divided Societies* edited by Desmond Rea (Gill and Macmillan, 1982).

For recent events and proposals I have drawn on the official proceedings of the New Ireland Forum (available from the Government Publications Sale Office in Dublin) and on the position papers of the Alliance party and the Unionist parties in Northern Ireland, and on the report to the Alliance parties in Great Britain of the committee chaired by Lord Donaldson. I have drawn heavily on drafts which I wrote as Vice-Chairman of the Independent Inquiry chaired by Lord Kilbrandon, whose report is obtainable from the British Irish Association. For the most recent events I have had to rely on newspaper reports, and I am particularly indebted to the excellent summary of happenings in Northern Ireland which appears in each issue of the periodical *Fortnight*. *Ireland: A Positive Proposal*, by Kevin Boyle and Tom Hadden, is a most valuable book, described in detail in Chapter 15 and quoted on p. 15.

1.

The Birth of Protestant Ulster

'To hell with the future, and long live the past
May God in his mercy look down on Belfast.'

This often quoted couplet encapsulates an important truth about the
politics of Northern Ireland, and indeed of the island of Ireland as a
whole. Everywhere in the world the politics of the present are condi-
tioned by the history of the past; but in Ireland in an especial manner
current political issues are interwoven and entangled with distant historical memories. In the political process in Northern Ireland recent
legislation and rising politicians are often less important than deeds
long done and men long dead. World wars begin and end, alliances
coalesce and crumble, empires wax and wane; the issues and the problems in Ulster retain their form unchanged as anniversaries and centen-
aries return. When the First World War ended, Winston Churchill
wrote:

> The whole map of Europe has been changed. . . . The mode and
> thought of men, the whole outlook on affairs, the grouping of
> parties, all have encountered violent and tremendous changes in
> the deluge of the world, but as the deluge subsides and the waters
> fall we see the dreary steeples of Fermanagh and Tyrone emerg-
> ing once again. The integrity of their quarrel is one of the few insti-
> tutions that has been left unaltered in the cataclysm which has
> swept the world.

Since then a second war has been fought, and the nations which slaugh-
tered each other in two wars now belong to a single European
community. But we have not yet brought peace to Fermanagh and
Tyrone, nor set to rest the ancient quarrels of Ulster.

1

To understand the confrontations of today, we must turn our minds back to the time when the distinction between Catholic and Protestant was a new thing, and some hoped might be a temporary thing.

In the reign of Elizabeth I the history of Ireland was a story of constant rebellion bloodily suppressed. England under Elizabeth, after a series of religious changes in previous reigns, had finally accepted the Protestant Reformation and thrown off the supremacy of the Pope. Those in England who retained the ancient faith were suspected — often with reason — of treason; the Queen's Irish subjects, resistant to Protestantism and rebellious against the Crown, were to be subjected to stern discipline on both political and religious grounds. Not for the last time, the English saw their ruthless treatment of the native population as essentially a civilising operation, imposing order on lawless anarchy. 'A barbarous country', said one of Elizabeth's officials, 'must first be broken by war before it will be capable of good government'.

Though the official Church of Ireland became, like the Church of England, a Protestant church, and though the bishoprics and cathedrals passed into Protestant hands, Protestantism made little progress among the people of Ireland. Only in the Pale, the fortified area around the capital City of Dublin, did the Reformation take root. The major part of the four provinces of Ireland — Ulster, Munster, Leinster and Connaught — remained resolutely Catholic. And it was in the northern-most province of Ulster that the Elizabethan Settlement was threatened by one of the most dangerous of the reign's rebellions. Hugh O'Neill, the Earl of Tyrone, rose in rebellion in 1595. In 1598 he inflicted a major defeat on an English army at the Battle of the Yellow Ford, near Armagh. In 1601 a fleet from Catholic Spain landed at Kinsale to offer help. O'Neill and his ally Hugh O'Donnell marched south to join the invaders. But Spaniards and Irishmen were defeated by the Protestant governor, Lord Mountjoy.

In 1603 Queen Elizabeth died and was succeeded by the Scots King James I. Tyrone, his power broken at the Battle of Kinsale, submitted to the Crown and was pardoned. He was allowed to keep his lands in Ulster, but four years later, with the Earl of Tyrconnel (Hugh O'Donnell's heir), he went into voluntary exile in France. On the lands forfeited by the fugitive Earls, colonies were planted — exclusively English and Scottish settlers, forbidden for the most part even to take

Irish tenants. The organisation of this new colony was entrusted to the City of London and its companies: the main city in the region, Derry, was renamed Londonderry.

While this official plantation was taking root in the western part of Ulster, another, unofficial influx of settlers was taking place in the eastern part of the province near Belfast. These eastern immigrants were Presbyterian Scots, dissenters from the Established Protestant church. The two settlements spread out to meet each other, but the demographic map of Northern Ireland reveals to this day the traces of the two original groupings. During the reign of James I, Ulster, which had been the last bastion of Catholic Gaelic Ireland in the fight against the Elizabethan Reformation, became the home of a substantial, determined and powerful Protestant colony.

The Ulster Catholics resented the loss of their lands to the newcomers, and under James's son Charles I they rose in revolt, not against the Crown, but against the Protestant settlers. The rebellion was bloody, and many thousand Protestants were killed. At Portadown, a hundred Protestant men, women and children were herded onto the town bridge and thrown into the river to drown or be knocked on the head as they tried to scramble ashore. Reports of Irish savagery were no doubt exaggerated in Protestant folklore, but it is hard to dismiss the contemporary evidence sworn soon after the events and now preserved in thirty-odd volumes in Trinity College, Dublin. The memory of the massacre of Portadown still lives in the minds of Ulster Unionists today.

Not only Protestants in Ireland remember the 1640s. The Irish Catholic rebels claimed to have no quarrel with King Charles I, and indeed they allied with the English Royalists against the Parliamentary forces in the Civil War. After the Royalists had been defeated in England, the Parliamentary general Cromwell crossed the Irish Sea to root out the King's last supporters and to punish the Irish rebels. His troops massacred the entire garrison, and many of the inhabitants, of the town of Drogheda, after a costly siege. The town of Wexford was stormed while a surrender was being negotiated, and two hundred women and children were reported killed in the market-place. Cromwell confiscated all Catholic land east of the Shannon, banished Irish landowners to the west, and distributed their property among his soldiers;

he was said to have sold Irish women to slavery in the West Indies. His name has remained, in Ireland, a byword for English brutality.

Throughout much of the seventeenth century Catholics in England and Ireland lived in hope that Britain might have a Catholic monarch. After Cromwell's death the son of Charles I was restored to the throne as Charles II: he was known to favour Catholics, but he did not himself become a Catholic until he was on his deathbed. His brother James II, however, was an open Catholic long before he became King in 1685. But his attempts to give Catholics freedom of conscience and a share of power in England were inept and self-defeating. He was driven out of England by the 'Glorious Revolution' of 1688 and the throne passed to his Dutch son-in-law, William of Orange. But as in the earlier Civil War the Irish remained loyal to the legitimate King longer than the English, and William was not acknowledged as King in Ireland until 1690.

When Ulster Protestants heard in 1688 that a Catholic King was being replaced by a Protestant one, their loyalty was divided. Rumours spread in Londonderry that the Catholics were planning a massacre similar to that of 1641. King James sent a new regiment to garrison the city: a Catholic regiment. The Protestant City authorities felt they had no choice but to admit the garrison: but on 7 December 1688 thirteen apprentice boys snatched the keys of the gates and locked them in the face of King James's troops. The town was besieged, and the King himself came in person to demand entry. The commander of the Protestant garrison, Lieutenant-Colonel Lundy, wanted to surrender the city, but the citizens rejected his authority and he had to flee in disguise. William of Orange sent a fleet with troops to relieve the city, but it remained idle in the River Foyle, on the other side of a boom placed by the besiegers. Thirty thousand people were locked in the city and thousands died of starvation. But demands for capitulation were met with the reply 'No surrender.' Finally, on 28 July 1689, the British ships broke through the boom and relieved the siege. William III followed across the Irish Sea, and routed the armies of King James at the Battle of the Boyne, on 12 July 1690. The Protestants were not only saved from massacre, they were established in dominion over the Catholic majority of Ireland.

The campaign of 1688–90 has left an indelible mark on the history and mythology of Northern Ireland. If Protestant Ulstermen gather in clubs called Orange Lodges, it is because William of Orange has ever afterwards been seen as a liberator from the tyranny of a Catholic king and the savagery of a Catholic mob. The action of the apprentice boys is commemorated by an annual march, and the anniversary of the Battle of the Boyne is marked by Protestant parades throughout the province. Any Protestant who is suspected of disloyalty to the Protestant cause is called a 'Lundy'; and the words 'No surrender' are repeated defiantly in response to any suggestion that the Protestant majority in Northern Ireland should share with the Catholics the power which their ancestors won from them in the heroic days of the Glorious Revolution.

2.

The Rise of Irish Nationalism

For most of the eighteenth century, Ireland was in a state of uneasy peace. Catholics were deprived of power and property by the Penal Laws: the practice of their religion was just barely permitted. One priest in each parish was allowed to say Mass; all members of religious orders — friars and monks — were banished. No Catholic could hold public office, practice any profession except medicine, stand for Parliament, vote, buy land, or even hold a long lease. Ninety-five per cent of the land passed into Protestant hands. While the Anglo-Irish ascendancy in Dublin produced works of literature, art and architecture that we admire to this day, much of the Catholic population sank into poverty and squalor, mocked by the Protestant establishment as dirty and slothful. The Penal Laws were described by Edmund Burke as

> a machine of wise and elaborate contrivance and as well fitted for the oppression, impoverishment and degradation of a people, and the debasement in them of human nature itself, as ever proceeded from the perverted ingenuity of man.

When, however, towards the end of the eighteenth century, Irish Nationalists began to seek a degree of independence from Britain, it was not the oppressed Catholics but the ascendant Protestants who took the lead. English statutes restraining Irish competition in trade were resented, particularly by the Presbyterians who had built up thriving industries in the north-east, and who in any case resented their disadvantages as dissenters. In the 1770s the rebellion of the American colonists against the mother country put thoughts of independence into the minds of the Protestant colonists in Ireland. A Dublin lawyer named Henry Grattan formed a Patriot party which sought to breathe new life into the moribund Irish Parliament. In 1782 the British Government, impressed by the formation of armed bands of Protestant 'Volunteers', conceded independence to the Irish Parliament under the British Crown. Henceforth, no laws were to be made for Ireland except by the King, Lords and Commons of Ireland itself, though Westminster continued to control Irish affairs by the exercise of patronage. Grattan's Parliament was essentially a Protestant affair, even after the Catholic Relief Act gave the franchise to some of the Catholic middle class. These early Irish Nationalists hardly spoke for any Irish nation as a whole.

After the French Revolution of 1789 it seemed, for a brief period, that Irishmen of all classes and sects might unite to establish a new independent nation embracing the whole island. Presbyterians from Belfast joined with others to found the Society of United Irishmen, recruiting Catholics, Presbyterians and Episcopalians. The Society's best-known member was a Dublin Protestant named Wolfe Tone, who described the movement's purposes thus:

> To subvert the tyranny of our execrable Government, to break the connection with England, the never failing source of our political evils, and to assert the Independence of my country — these were my objects. To unite the whole of Ireland, to abolish the memory of all past dissensions . . . these were my means.

Tone was the first Irish Republican, and he sought help from revolutionary France. An armada sailed to Ireland in 1796, but could not land at Bantry Bay. The United Irishmen were stamped out by ruthless military action in Ulster, and many Ulster Protestants formed a sectarian Orange Order in opposition to them. Elsewhere sporadic revolts broke out, and the rebels won occasional successes in battle. But they also committed atrocities which imperilled the unity among the sects. When they were finally defeated by government forces at the Battle of Vinegar Hill in 1798, a terrible vengeance was taken on them and their supporters. General Abercrombie, sent from England to take command, resigned in protest at the troops' excesses.

The upshot of the revolt of the United Irishmen was not an independent Ireland, but the Act of Union of 1800. This Act extinguished the Irish Parliament, and provided instead seats in the Westminster Parliament in which Irishmen would be in a permanent minority. Irish nationalists regarded the Act of Union as a piece of trickery, pushed through by corruption. Thus the Union Jack, the flag which was created to symbolise the Act of Union, has since been an object of hatred to Irish Nationalists. They saw it not simply as the emblem of an occupying power, but as a permanent memento of an act of English perfidy.

One further attempt at rebellion was made during this period of revolutionary fervour. In 1803 a young Dubliner named Robert Emmett planned to seize Dublin Castle and proclaim a Republic. But a succession of accidents alerted the Government to the plot, and the few followers whom Emmett managed to assemble got out of control. Seventeen of the conspirators were executed, and Emmett was hanged in Dublin. His speech from the dock has been endlessly quoted. 'When my country takes her place among the nations of the earth, then, and not till then, let my epitaph be written.' To this day, Irish Nationalists debate whether the time has come to write Emmett's epitaph.

The next Irish leader to leave a name to history and mythology was no revolutionary. Daniel O'Connell founded the broadly-based and pacific Catholic Association: he stood for Parliament in 1828 and was elected for Clare. In 1829 he succeeded in obtaining the Act of Emancipation which removed the ban which prevented him and his fellow Catholics from taking seats in Parliament. He then devoted himself to a campaign for the repeal of the Act of Union, and had considerable success in assembling 'Monster Meetings' of Irishmen in peaceful protest against the Act. The campaign had not achieved its goal at the time of his death in 1847, and by then political matters had been overshadowed by a terrible famine in Ireland. This reduced the population from eight and a half million to six and a half million in six years. About one million died and the remainder emigrated, to be followed by many others during the century, so that by 1900 the population of the island had decreased to about four million.

The British Government was not wholly indifferent to the sufferings of the Irish during the famine, but the relief it offered was ineffective, hampered by the dogmas of laissez-faire economics. Moreover, though failure of the potato crop, which provided the food of the poor, was due to natural causes, there was grain in abundance which could have fed many of the victims had it not been claimed by landlords as rent and sent abroad. It was no wonder that the famine left a new legacy of hatred towards England, a hatred carried overseas, especially to the United States, by those who emigrated to escape starvation. Resentment at the Government's heartlessness led to a new revolt in 1848, the year when the tide of revolution rose high throughout Europe. The Young Ireland Movement, led once again by well-to-do Protestants, organised a brief abortive uprising. Its legacy to Irish Nationalists was the tricolour, the green, white and orange flag presented to Young Ireland by French Republicans which is now the national flag of the Republic of Ireland.

Survivors of the 1848 rising founded, ten years later, the Irish Republican Brotherhood, a secret, oathbound, society dedicated to the establishment of an Irish Republic. Its members called themselves Fenians, from the name of a legendary Irish hero. The Fenian rising of 1867 was no more successful than its predecessors. Many of the leaders of the movement were in English prisons; an attempt to rescue some of them by blowing up the wall of Clerkenwell prison led to an explosion in which twelve people were killed and fifty injured.

3.

Home Rule to Republic

Once again, a series of revolutionary failures paved the way for more successful movement for reform by constitutional means. Under the leadership of Charles Stewart Parnell, a Protestant landowner, elected MP for Meath in 1875, Irish constitutional nationalists began to campaign for Home Rule, or self-government under the British Crown. In 1879 another famine threatened Ireland, and tenant farmers, losing out in competition with newly imported cheap American grain, fell behind with their rents and were threatened with eviction. A Fenian named Michael Davitt founded a Land League to demand a national reduction of rents and an end to evictions: Parnell became its president. The Liberal Government of W. E. Gladstone was persuaded to pass the Land Act of 1881 which gave security of tenure and set up courts to assess fair rents. By 1885 Gladstone himself had become a partisan of Home Rule, but the Bill which he introduced for this purpose in 1886 ran into stiff opposition.

The measure was opposed by the Conservative party *en masse*, and many Liberals deserted their Government to defend the Union. The Conservative Lord Randolph Churchill declared that the Orange card was the card to play: the Orange Order lodges in the North of Ireland should be mobilised against Home Rule. There were those in the North who threatened civil war. 'Ulster will fight', said Lord Randolph in Belfast. 'And Ulster will be right.' There was no need for Ulster to fight, because the Bill was defeated in the House of Commons. In the ensuing celebrations in Belfast Catholics were killed. Parliament was dissolved, and the Conservatives returned to power under Lord Salisbury; but of the Irish members returned, eighty-six out of a hundred and three were supporters of Home Rule. Parnell was discredited as leader of his party when he was cited as co-respondent in a divorce case and denounced by the Irish Catholic bishops. He died, a broken man, in 1891. Gladstone's Liberals won an election in 1882 with a sufficiently large majority to carry a second Home Rule Bill. But after it had passed the Commons in 1893 the Bill was rejected by the Lords. A year later Gladstone retired, with the Irish Parliamentary party in disarray and Home Rule seemingly a lost cause. Unionists rejoiced. They had feared that Home Rule would imperil Ulster's prosperity by cutting it off from English markets; the civil and religious liberties of Protestants would be unsafe in an overwhelmingly Catholic island. Home Rule, they argued, would be Rome Rule.

'No man', Parnell had said, 'can set bounds to the march of a nation', and in the very year of the defeat of the second Home Rule Bill there was a significant development in Irish nationalism. Douglas Hyde, a scholar and poet, founded the Gaelic League, with the object of reviving the native Irish language and literature, and creating a distinctively Irish culture. It was non-sectarian and non-political, but its ethos inspired revolutionary nationalists. The Republican poet Padraic Pearse wrote, in 1903, 'The Gaelic League will be recognised in history as the most revolutionary influence that has ever come into Ireland'. Pearse and his friends were no longer content with the goal of Home Rule under the British Crown, they looked forward to the setting up of an Irish Republic. The Irish Republican Brotherhood, small and ineffective since the failed Fenian rising, took on new life in 1898, the centenary of the United Irishmen's rising.

At the turn of the century, however, most politically active Irishmen were not yet Republicans. Arthur Griffith, a journalist, founded in 1899 a newspaper called *The United Irishman* and in 1905 an organisation called Sinn Fein ('We ourselves'). This urged that Irish MPs should withdraw from Westminster and form an Irish Parliament and Government, subject to the British Crown but otherwise independent. The Irish Parliamentary party, under John Redmond, succeeded in obtaining a series of reforms, the Land Purchase Acts, by which the State bought out landlords in Ireland and offered mortgages to the sitting tenants. But no progress was made on the issue of Home Rule until 1910 when, in two elections, the balance of power was held by the eighty-two Irish nationalist members.

Asquith's Liberal Government, by the Parliament Act of 1911, abolished the veto of the House of Lords; the third Home Rule Bill then passed through Parliament in 1912. But Ulster Protestants were determined that it should never come into force. In 1912 half a million Protestants, under the leadership of Sir Edward Carson, signed a 'Solemn League and Covenant' to use 'all means which may be found necessary to defeat the present conspiracy to set up a Home Rule Parliament in Ireland'. Conservative British leaders pledged their support. An Ulster Volunteer Force was founded, 100,000 strong, to resist Home Rule by force of arms. It drilled at first with dummy wooden rifles, but by 1914 24,000 rifles and 3,000,000 rounds of ammunition had been smuggled in. A provisional Government was formed to take power if Home Rule was introduced. Sixty officers of the British Army garrisoned in Ireland announced that they would accept dismissal rather than obey orders to coerce the Ulstermen. But elsewhere in Ireland, an unofficial force of Irish Volunteers was set up as a counterweight to the UVF. They too began to smuggle arms, and a consignment was brought in from Germany, by Sir Roger Casement and Erskine Childers, a few days before the outbreak of the First World War in 1914.

The Home Rule Act went onto the statute book in September 1914, but its operation was suspended until the war ended. Before it came into force, an Amending Bill was to be introduced to deal with the special position of Ulster. Meanwhile, the UVF and the great majority of the Irish Volunteers agreed to support the Crown and to fight for Britain in the war. Ulster regiments formed from the UVF fought with great gallantry: at the Somme in July 1916 in two days the 36th Ulster division suffered 5,500 losses and won four Victoria Crosses. Many Southern Irish soldiers also fought bravely beside the British; but a radical anti-war minority of Irish Volunteers remained at home. At Easter 1916 some of these under Padraic Pearse, joined hands with James Connolly's 'Irish Citizen Army', veterans of pre-war labour struggles, to stage a rising in Dublin which proclaimed an Irish Republic from the steps of the GPO. The rising was generally unpopular at the time, and no more than 1800 people were involved. The German rifles which were to arm the rebels were intercepted, and the rebellion was put down within a week by the British Army. But the subsequent execution of Pearse, Connolly and thirteen other leaders of the rising — a small proportion of the numbers who had been involved

in armed rebellion in the midst of a war that took the lives of millions —
was bitterly resented in Ireland, and converted many moderate citizens
into convinced nationalists. 'Out of the ashes of the 1916 rising', a historian has written, 'grew the Irish Republican Army.'

Many of those imprisoned for their part in the Easter Rising were
released by Christmas 1916. One of these, Michael Collins, reorganised
the Volunteers around an IRB network: his group joined with the Sinn
Fein movement of Arthur Griffith under the presidency of another
newly-released commandant of the rising, Eamon de Valera. Sinn Fein
stood for a much greater degree of Irish independence than was conceded by the still unimplemented Home Rule Act of 1914; it wanted to
sever all connection with the British Crown and perpetuate the Republic proclaimed in 1916. Its methods, initially and overtly, were non-
violent and constitutional. Sinn Fein candidates defeated Parliamentary
party candidates in a number of by-elections in 1917, and in the General
Election shortly after the Armistice in 1918 the party won nearly three-
quarters of the Irish seats. The majority of those thus elected met in
Dublin, proclaimed themselves Dáil Eireann, or the Irish Parliament,
and declared Ireland an independent Republic, with Da Valera as its
first President.

4.

Troubles, Treaty and Partition

Before the Dail's proclamations were turned into reality, much blood was to flow. Many Republicans became convinced that only force of arms would drive British authority out of Ireland. Collins organised the IRA in a systematic campaign to kill policemen of the Royal Irish Constabulary. The police retaliated ruthlessly, and reinforcements were brought from across the Irish Sea: ex-army officers, known as Auxiliaries, and other ranks, known from their improvised uniforms as Black and Tans. The brutal methods which the 'Tans' adopted in response to IRA atrocities served to make British rule ever more unpopular. Typical of the ruthlessness of the two sides to the conflict were the events of 'Bloody Sunday', 21 November 1920. Early in the morning fourteen British intelligence officers were shot in their beds by Collins's agents. In reprisal the same afternoon the army sprayed a Dublin football crowd with machine-gun and rifle fire, and in the evening three Sinn Feiners were murdered in Dublin Castle. By the time a truce was called between the IRA and the Crown forces in July 1921, it was estimated that 752 had been killed and 866 wounded on the Irish side.

During these 'Troubles' in the South, the North of Ireland had been given its own Parliament and Government. The British Prime Minister, Lloyd George, had become convinced that the partition of the island was the only solution to the problems that had prevented the implementation of Home Rule in 1914. His Coalition Government in 1920 replaced the Home Rule Act with the Government of Ireland Act. This set up two Irish Parliaments, one for the six Northern counties of Antrim, Armagh, Down, Fermanagh, Londonderry, and Tyrone, with the cities of Belfast and Londonderry; the other for the remaining twenty-six counties of Southern Ireland. Each Parliament was to consist of a Senate and a Commons which was to be elected by Proportional

14

Representation. Revenue was to be raised by taxes collected by Westminster and allotted to the two parts of Ireland: it was to be spent by local governments who would have power over law and order, local government, education, social services, agriculture, industry and internal trade. Ultimate sovereignty rested with the Westminster Parliament, which retained power over 'excepted matters', such as the Crown, the armed forces, the coinage and external trade. The Parliaments were enabled to send representatives to an All-Ireland Council; if the two Parliaments decided to unite, further powers would be transferred from Westminster. All members of both Parliaments were to swear allegiance to the King.

The 1920 Act never became effective in the South, but it provided the Constitution of Northern Ireland until the 1970s. The partition which it imposed was bitterly resented by Irish nationalists, some of whom claim to this day that the Act is the cause of all the continuing troubles in Northern Ireland. But it is quite wrong to suggest that all the problems arise from the constitutional arrangements of 1920 which divided Ireland. The tensions between the Protestant and Roman Catholic communities had existed long before. In the words of a recent respected historian of Northern Ireland, 'Partition was, in fact, no deep-laid plot on the part of Britain to divide Irishmen and retain Ireland in its clutches. It was simply a recognition of reality. Irishmen were divided before partition: partition merely recognised, though ultimately accentuated, those divisions' (P. Buckland, *A History of Northern Ireland*, p. 21).

The matter has been very well put by two distinguished Irish lawyers, one from Northern Ireland and one from the Republic of Ireland.

> The truth in crude terms is that both the Republic of Ireland and Northern Ireland were created by a combination of military force and popular will. The idea of partition was first seriously raised when it became clear that very large numbers of Protestants were prepared to fight in Carson's UVF against the imposition of home rule by Britain on an all-Ireland basis. The idea that the rest of Ireland must be granted a measure of independence was similarly accepted when it became clear that the IRA could not be defeated

and that the vast majority of voters in the twenty-six counties supported the objectives of Sinn Fein. It is true that the British government made no attempt to coerce the Unionists and that it did its best to suppress the IRA. It is also true that the adoption of partition as a solution, however temporary, may be attributed to other contemporary British political and defence concerns. It is nonetheless essential to remember that the underlying reasons for partition were that the vast majority of the inhabitants in the North and in the South of Ireland had expressed incompatible loyalties and commitments, and that very large numbers in each part had shown their willingness to fight for those commitments.

But if partition was inevitable, the way it was carried out was not, and the drawing of the border, and the way in which it was brought into force, was seen by nationalists as unfair and dishonest. There were three ways in which the border might have been drawn: to include all nine counties of the historic province of Ulster; to include the six counties of the present province; or to include merely the four counties of Antrim, Armagh, Down and Londonderry. A four-county province would have included the great majority of the Protestants, and would have been the most acceptable to nationalists; but it might have been economically unviable. A nine-county province would have contained only a small and precarious Protestant majority. It was the six-county province which contained the largest area with a safe majority. Its creation, therefore, was seen as a triumph for Unionists, though there was something of a paradox in the fact that the Act of 1920 should give Home Rule to the group which had been the most determined opponents of Home Rule. In July 1921 King George V opened the Parliament in Belfast, and Sir James Craig became Prime Minister.

The Anglo-Irish Treaty of 1921, which brought to an end the guerilla war between the IRA and the Crown forces, provided for the six-county Northern Ireland to remain in the United Kingdom, but article 12 provided for a Boundary Commission to be set up to examine and adjust the frontiers between the two parts of Ireland, in accordance with the wishes of the inhabitants, but also in the light of economic and geographical considerations. Nationalists confidently hoped that the Boundary Commission would recommend the transfer of large portions of Northern Ireland to the South. But in fact the issue of partition was not the major item on the agenda during the discussions which turned the truce of July 1921 into the Treaty of December 1921.

De Valera remained in Dublin while an Irish delegation led by Arthur Griffith and Michael Collins negotiated with Lloyd George and the British Cabinet. The upshot of the deliberations was that Ireland was given dominion status, with its own army and navy and control of its own affairs, on the model of the Canadian Constitution: it was to be called the Irish Free State. The six counties were given one month to opt out of the Free State if they wished: if they did — as they certainly would — a Boundary Commission would be necessary to determine the border in its final form. All members of the Free State Dail were to swear loyalty in the following words:

> I do solemnly swear true faith and allegiance to the Constitution of the Irish Free State . . . and that I will be faithful to HM King George V . . . in virtue of the common citizenship of Ireland with Great Britain and her adherence to and membership of the group of nations forming the British Commonwealth of nations.

Despite the qualified form of this oath of allegiance, it was regarded by many members of the IRA as the negation of what they had fought for. De Valera himself disowned the Treaty, and it was ratified in the Dail only by a small majority. A general election in June 1922 returned a majority in support of the Treaty, but in the same month fighting broke out between the new Free State army and those members of the old IRA who had refused to acknowledge the authority of the new Government led by Griffith and Collins. Meanwhile in the North the proposal for a Boundary Commission had reawakened Protestant fears, and bloody riots occurred. In Belfast during the six months after the Treaty came into force 236 people were killed, about two-thirds of them Catholics: the dead were victims both of Unionist brutality and of indiscriminate IRA attacks. The newly formed Ulster Special Constabulary, sectarian and undisciplined, acquired a fearsome reputation among Catholics. Especially hated were the part-time constables or 'B specials'.

In the South the civil war between pro-Treaty and anti-Treaty forces was brief but bitter. Many on both sides were killed by those who had been their comrades in arms in the Republican struggle against

England. Collins was killed in an ambush in August 1922. A draconian Emergency Powers Act was introduced by the Free State Government under William Cosgrave, who had succeeded to the Premiership when Griffith died of a heart attack. In November and December Erskine Childers and two leaders of the old IRA, Rory O'Connor and Liam Mellows, were executed by the Free State Government. By the time De Valera ordered the anti-Treaty forces to lay down their arms, in May 1923, seventy-seven men had been shot by the Free State Government (more than three times as many as were executed by the British during the troubles of 1920–1). Thirteen thousand Republicans served terms in Free State prisons. The Free State Government, under William Cosgrave, faced an appalling task in trying to unite and consolidate the new nation. It had little energy or stomach for forcing the issue of the border.

When the Boundary Commission finally met, it disappointed nationalists by recommending only very minor adjustments to the six-county line. Even these modest recommendations were never put into effect. Cosgrave accepted the existing line in exchange for financial amendments to the Treaty. The boundary was confirmed by a tripartite agreement between the British, Free State and Northern Ireland Governments, and the agreement was lodged with the League of Nations.

5.

A Catholic State and a Protestant State

While the Free State Government stamped out those elements of the IRA who had not obeyed the order to dump arms, De Valera himself organised the Sinn Feiners who had remained loyal to him into a new party to which he gave the name Fianna Fail (Warriors of Ireland). Founded in 1926, the party won forty-four seats in a General Election in the following year; it was not, however, until 1932 that it secured a majority in the Dail. Once in power, De Valera and his party set about altering the Treaty provisions in the direction of complete independence. He suspended payments to the British exchequer, reduced the role of the Governor General and abolished the oath of allegiance.

In 1937 a new Constitution was drawn up for the twenty-six-county state. Articles 2 and 3 of that constitution read:

> Article 2. The national territory consists of the whole island of Ireland, its islands and the territorial seas.

> Article 3. Pending the re-integration of the national territory, and without prejudice to the right of the Parliament and Government established by this Constitution to exercise jurisdiction over the whole of that territory, the laws enacted by that Parliament shall have the like area and extent of application as the laws of Saorstat Eireann (i.e. the twenty-six-county Free State) and the like extra-territorial effect.

These articles were seen by Unionists in the North as an insolent claim to territory which by international law was part of another State, and a

19

perfidious renunciation of undertakings given by the Irish Government in 1925.

Another article, article 44, gave further strength to Protestant determination to have no truck with a United Ireland. It read:

> The State recognises the special position of the Holy Catholic Apostolic and Roman Church as the guardian of the faith professed by the great majority of its citizens.

Though article 44 of De Valera's constitution was replaced thirty-five years later, articles 2 and 3 remain in the Constitution. Their contemporary effect within the legal system of the Republic today is a matter of some controversy. According to a decision of the Irish Supreme Court in 1977, 'The national claim to unity exists not in the legal but in the political order.' Professor John Kelly's authoritative work *The Irish Constitution* sums up the present effect of the articles thus:

> It would seem that (1) as a political statement, Articles 2 and 3 deny the legitimacy of Northern Ireland as an entity withdrawn from the jurisdiction of the Oireachtas (Parliament) and Government established by the Constitution; (2) as a legal statement, they have the effect of preventing an acknowledgement, by any authority (such as the Oireachtas or the Government) subject to control on constitutional criteria, amounting to an admission of any *de jure* status for the dispensation under which Northern Ireland exists; (3) concomitantly, they may even leave open some room for asserting that the State in theory comprehends all of Ireland, notwithstanding that it exercises no jurisdiction in Northern Ireland; but (4) that — so to speak, on a less fundamentalist, 'working' level of legality — they allow both Oireachtas and courts to treat Northern Ireland as lawfully existing.

The 1937 Constitution did not declare Ireland a Republic. That did not happen until a decade later, after the Second World War. In 1938 Chamberlain's British Government gave up the 1921 Treaty rights to naval use of Irish ports — a surrender bitterly regretted by Churchill and his admirals during the wartime years. The Irish policy during the war, under a Fianna Fail Government, was one of strict neutrality between Britain and Germany. It was carried so far that in 1945 De

Valera called on the German ambassador to offer his condolences on the
death of Hitler. In 1948, after sixteen years rule, the Fianna Fail
Government was replaced by a coalition headed by John Costello of
Fine Gael, the party which had inherited the tradition of Cosgrave and
the first Free State governments. It was this coalition government
which renamed the Irish state 'The Republic of Ireland' and withdrew
from the British Commonwealth.

In response, the British Government of Attlee passed the Northern
Ireland Act of 1949 which regulated the relations between the United
Kingdom and the new Republic. It contained the following statement,
the first version of the famous 'guarantee' to Ulster Unionists.

> Parliament hereby declares that Northern Ireland remains part of
> His Majesty's Dominions and of the United Kingdom and affirms
> that in no event will Northern Ireland or any part thereof cease to
> be part of His Majesty's Dominions and of the United Kingdom
> without the consent of the Parliament of Northern Ireland.

Northern Protestants had not wanted the Home Rule that they were
given in 1921, but in the years since the creation of the six-county
province they had lived reasonably contentedly under their Government at Stormont. They boasted of living in a Protestant State with a
Protestant Parliament. In the twelve Stormont elections between 1921
and 1969 Unionists never won fewer than forty of the fifty-two seats.
The half-million Catholics locked by partition into subjection to the one
million Protestants were not similarly happy, though armed resistance
to the state in the North soon dwindled and by the beginning of 1926 all
internees and political prisoners had been released.

Catholic nationalists claim that the fifty years of Stormont rule were a
period of exclusively Unionist power and privilege under which Catholics suffered systematic discrimination. Recent historians who have
striven to be impartial accept this claim, with some qualification. Thus,
Patrick Buckland, in his *History of Northern Ireland*, writes:

> The Unionist regime was neither as vindictive nor as oppressive as
> regimes elsewhere in the world with problems of compact or irre-
> dentist minorities. The fact remains that, owing to local condi-
> tions, the power of the government was used in the interests of

Unionists and Protestants, with scant regard for the interests of the region as a whole or for the claims and susceptibilities of the substantial minority. (p. 72)

Professor John Whyte, after examining in detail allegations of unfairness in electoral practices, public employment, policing, private employment, public housing, and regional policy, and having dismissed some of the more extreme charges, finds that most of the proven cases of discrimination occurred in the west of the province. He then says in conclusion:

> Elsewhere, discrimination occurred. The USC was everywhere a Protestant militia; some police decisions displayed partisanship; there were fewer Catholics in the higher reaches of the public service than were willing and qualified to serve; some public firms discriminated against Catholics. But when all this is said the prominence of an area in the west remains. There, the greyness of the picture over most of the province changes to an ominous darkness. The Unionist government must bear its share of responsibility. It put through the original gerrymander which underpinned so many of the subsequent malpractices, and then, despite repeated protests, did nothing to stop those malpractices continuing. The most serious charge against the Northern Ireland government is not that it was directly responsible for widespread discrimination, but that it allowed discrimination on such a scale over a substantial segment of Northern Ireland.

A particularly flagrant example of the gerrymandering which underpinned discriminatory malpractice was offered by the city of Londonderry. The city's population was roughly three-fifths Catholic and two-fifths Unionist. But large numbers of Catholics were concentrated in overlarge electoral districts, while Protestants were placed in smaller ones. The effect was that there was regularly a Protestant majority of twelve to eight on the city corporation. Moreover, owing to the allocation of extra votes to those with substantial property qualifications, Protestants could muster more votes per head than Catholics could. The Proportional Representation provided for in the Government of Ireland Act of 1920 had been abolished by Stormont for local elections; and the Westminster Government did nothing to implement the clause in that Act which had forbidden discrimination on religious grounds. The effect of Protestant privilege was seen in discrimination in the allocation of houses and jobs.

By the 1960s, however, the Government of Northern Ireland had a number of solid achievements to point to. An IRA campaign in the border areas between 1956–1962 was quietly and effectively subdued by the Royal Ulster Constabulary. The Catholic Nationalist party was persuaded to accept the role of official opposition, and thus ended Catholic boycotts of the province's institutions. The economy was expanding while the province was relatively stable and tranquil. Infant mortality had been brought down to 23 per thousand from near 100 per thousand in the twenties; unemployment was down to about 6 per cent.

The Kilbrandon Commission on the Constitution visited Northern Ireland in 1970 to take evidence about the working of devolved government. Its members found strong support for Home Rule in the province from witnesses of widely differing political views: they reported that no organised body of opinion had suggested that it should be abolished. They found evidence of substantial advantages from administrative devolution, and aside from sectarian issues they found that powers of devolved legislation had been constructively used, adapting and often improving on Westminster legislation. The Commission summed up the advantages of Home Rule. In areas unaffected by sectarian problems, it said,

> . . . conspicuous progress was made under it. Perhaps the most impressive of these was in the field of health, where Northern Ireland, which used to be well below the standards of Great Britain, caught up with and in some respects surpassed them. The other social services were steadily built up. Education was greatly improved and though it still continues, below university level, in two almost entirely different systems, both are supported by the state. Economic policy was flexible and imaginative, and, though the level of unemployment continued to be higher than the average for Great Britain, the gap had been significantly narrowed. (p. 380)

But the Commission noted defects of the Stormont system: its bicameral legislature was overelaborate, and its financial arrangements were too strictly controlled by the U.K. Treasury. Above all,

The institutions were of a kind which left a large section of the community always in a minority, without any share in government or any prospect of securing a share in government, and the restrictions placed on the exercise of the devolved functions did not suffice to safeguard the interests of that minority. (p. 381)

It was this fact which led to the train of events which brought down the institutions in question. From 1963 the Government of Captain Terence O'Neill, adopted a new and conciliatory attitude to Catholics. O'Neill visited Catholic institutions in the North and invited to Stormont the Irish Prime Minister (Sean Lemass, who had succeeded De Valera as leader of Fianna Fail in 1959). Even these modest gestures stirred up voluble Protestant opposition, led by a demagogic Presbyterian minister named Ian Paisley. Catholics in 1967 formed a Civil Rights Movement for Northern Ireland, modelled on the National Council for Civil Liberties in Britain and on the movement led by Martin Luther King among America's black citizens. Its initial aims were modest: one man one vote in council elections; fair allocation of housing; anti-discrimination machinery; and the disbandment of the B specials. The first demonstration of the movement was a march to Dungannon, on 28 August 1968, to protest against housing discrimination by the Unionist Rural District Council.

6.

Dungannon to Sunningdale

The Civil Rights Movement was non-violent, and its first march passed off peaceably. But in October protesters paraded more provocatively through Protestant areas of Londonderry in spite of a government ban. The march was opposed by Paisley's supporters and other Unionists and was broken up with excessive violence by the police. Seventy-eight civilians were injured, as well as eighteen policemen. A protest group called the Derry Citizens' Action Committee was set up by a Londonderry teacher named John Hume. At Queen's University in Belfast some 3000 students enrolled in a radical organisation, People's Democracy, whose aims soon went far beyond the demands of the Civil Rights Movement. Though a number of Protestant paramilitary organisations had been formed in reaction to O'Neill's reforms and the Civil Rights Movement, the IRA was still inactive and insignificant.

In January 1969 People's Democracy organised a march from Belfast to Derry. The march was legal and non-violent, but police sent to cover it joined Unionist mobs in attacking it before and after it reached Londonderry. In the Catholic area of the Bogside, a Government Report later found that policemen 'were guilty of misconduct which involved assault and battery, malicious damage to property . . . and the use of provocative, sectarian and political slogans'.

The events of January undid the good effect of a package of local government reforms which O'Neill had offered late in 1968 aimed especially at ending housing discrimination. Catholics became impatient and Protestants alarmed. O'Neill called an election in February, but it failed to strengthen his position and he resigned in April to be succeeded by Major James Chichester-Clark. The election marked the end of the old Nationalist party: its leader's seat, in Londonderry, went to John Hume.

25

The summer 'marching season' of 1969 was marked by horrific violence. The Protestant Apprentice Boys of Derry marched into the Bogside on 12 August; they were greeted with stones and petrol bombs thrown by Catholics behind siege barriers. Police retaliated violently and fighting went on until troops of the British Army came between the two sides on 14 August. Two days later Protestants from the Shankill area in Belfast made armed attacks on Catholics in the Falls area. Once again the police, in particular the B specials, showed themselves brutally partisan, and once again the British Army had to intervene to restore an uneasy peace. After nights in which six people had been killed and 150 Catholic homes burnt, the soldiers were welcomed by the Catholics as protectors.

These four days in August 1969 brought the troubles of Northern Ireland to the attention of the world. In Dublin the Prime Minister, Jack Lynch, who had succeeded Lemass, broadcast that the Irish Government could no longer stand idly by to see innocent people injured: field hospitals would be set up on the Border. 'Re-unification of the national territory can provide the only permanent solution for the problem.' In England, Prime Minister Wilson, with ministers summoned from Northern Ireland, issued the Downing Street Declaration:

> Every citizen of Northern Ireland is entitled to the same equality of treatment and freedom from discrimination as obtains in the rest of the United Kingdom, irrespective of political views or religion.

Between 1969 and 1972 a large number of reforms were indeed passed. The Electoral Law Act of 1969 provided for adult suffrage in local elections; the ratepayer's franchise was abolished. All local government boundaries and wards were redrawn. A Parliamentary Ombudsman and a Commissioner for Complaints were appointed. Following a report by the explorer Lord Hunt, the Royal Ulster Constabulary was thoroughly overhauled. The force was disarmed, and a new representative police authority set up: the Ulster Special Constabulary was abolished, and a new part-time security force, the Ulster Defence Regiment, was set up within the British Army; the police role in prosecutions was modified and later replaced by an independent Director of Public Prosecutions for Northern Ireland. A Ministry of Community Relations was set up, and also an independent Community

Relations Commission. The 1970 Prevention of Incitement to Hatred
Act contained the equivalent of the criminal provisions of the English
Race Relations Act of 1965. In 1971 a Housing Executive was set up to
deal with public authority housebuilding and to allocate houses on an
objective points system.

These substantial reforms did not, however, succeed in stemming the
tide of violence. On the contrary, violence became more widespread
and systematic as the dormant IRA re-awoke to life. The IRA had
exploded a few bombs in Belfast in April 1969, but at that time their
activities were eclipsed by the more substantial bombing campaign of
the Protestant UVF. Since 1962 official thinking in the IRA had been
moving away from violence towards left-wing political action. After the
rioting in the ghettos in 1969 a group of Belfast members broke away
from the Marxist-minded 'Officials' (or 'stickies') and formed the
Provisional IRA (the 'provos'). The two groups were hostile and
sometimes fought each other. The Provisionals gradually became the
dominant partners in the 'armed struggle': it was in February 1971 that
they killed their first British soldier.

By this time the British Army, by heavy-handed implementation of
security measures, provoked indeed by reckless rioting, had lost the
confidence initially enjoyed among the Catholic community. A three-
day curfew imposed on the Falls Road in summer 1970 alienated many
in the ghettos. The troubles began to take on the form of a guerilla war
between the Army and the PIRA.

Besides the split between the two wings of the IRA, the year 1970
saw the emergence of two other groups who sought Catholic support.
The Social Democratic and Labour Party united constitutional nation-
alist survivors of a number of earlier parties, such as Gerry Fitt and
Paddy Devlin from a Catholic labour background, and John Hume and
Austin Currie, younger men who had come into prominence during the
Civil Rights Movement. The Alliance party, under Oliver Napier, was
non-sectarian and sought to appeal to both Catholics and Protestants.
Both parties had seats at Stormont, though the SDLP withdrew in July
1971 following two shootings by the British Army in Londonderry.

The last Prime Minister of Northern Ireland was Brian Faulkner,
who succeeded Chichester-Clark in March 1971. Faulkner pressed
ahead with the programme of reform. His measures alienated many

members of his own party, who formed new groupings around his Unionist critics. The group which was to be significant for the future was the Democratic Unionist Party formed in September 1971 by Ian Paisley. But proposals for reform came to seem less and less significant as the toll of terrorism and counter-terrorism mounted. In 1971 114 civilians were killed and 1838 injured; the security forces lost 59 dead and 707 injured. In an offensive aimed at the breakdown of government, the PIRA maimed and murdered civilians as well as Crown forces.

The Government's response was to introduce internment without trial for those suspected of connection with terrorism. In a dawn swoop in August some 350 people were arrested, and by the end of 1971 the internment camps held something like 700, more than at any time since 1921. Some of those thus taken into custody were interrogated by harsh methods which, though they did not amount to torture, were later found by the European Court of Human Rights to be 'inhuman and degrading'. Many of those arrested were innocent people, and the tough security measures increased Catholic alienation from the Stormont regime. As a protest against internment, Catholic leaders organised a rent and rates strike, and four local councils refused to discharge their functions. The climax of disaffection came on another 'Bloody Sunday' in January 1972 when after an illegal and provocative protest march thirteen people were shot dead in the Bogside by British paratroopers. In the nationalist backlash, the British Embassy in Dublin was burnt down. A bomb was placed by the Official IRA in the officers' mess of the paratroopers in Aldershot killing five cleaners, a chaplain and a gardener. The crowded Abercorn restaurant in Belfast was bombed, causing the death of two women and injuring another 130 innocent shoppers.

After these incidents the British Prime Minister Heath decided to recall law and order powers to Westminster. Faulkner and his colleagues resigned, the Stormont Government and Parliament was suspended and Direct Rule was imposed from Westminster. William Whitelaw became the first Secretary of State for Northern Ireland, and henceforth Northern Ireland legislation was introduced by unamendable Orders in Council.

Whitelaw aimed to conciliate Catholics: he greatly reduced the number of internees, and offered paramilitary prisoners a special category status. The Official IRA declared an unconditional ceasefire; the Provisionals offered a truce in June and six leaders held talks in London under safe-conduct. Before any conclusion was reached, the PIRA called off the truce and launched one of its most horrific attacks in Belfast on 'Bloody Friday' (21 July), killing eleven people and maiming 130. As an alternative to internment without trial, a Committee under Lord Diplock recommended that terrorists should be tried by judges sitting alone, without juries who could be subjected to intimidation. Internment was to be phased out, and apart from arrangements for interim custody, commitment without trial was to be replaced by conviction and sentencing by Diplock courts.

Heath's Government regarded Direct Rule as a temporary measure and made strenuous efforts to explore other options. A constitutional conference was held at Darlington in 1972, but only half the Irish parties attended, and both the SDLP and the DUP stayed away.

To reassure the Unionist majority, a plebiscite about the border was held on 8 March 1973. Only 600,000 of the one million voters went to the polls, but of these 592,000 voted to remain in the United Kingdom. A few weeks later the Government published a white paper offering to restore devolved government on condition that executive power was shared between representatives of both majority and minority communities. The White Paper spoke also of 'the Irish Dimension' — the community of interests linking Northern Ireland to the Irish Republic.

The Northern Ireland Assembly Act, in May 1973, provided for a single-chamber Assembly of seventy-eight members to be elected by the single transferable vote system of proportional representation. More far-reaching was the Northern Ireland Constitution Act, passed in July, which still provides the basis of the constitutional arrangements in Northern Ireland. The Act begins by a reaffirmation of the Guarantee of 1949, in altered form to take account of the disappearance of the Stormont Parliament.

> It is hereby declared that Northern Ireland remains part of Her Majesty's dominions and of the United Kingdom, and it is hereby affirmed that in no event will Northern Ireland or any part of it cease to be part of Her Majesty's dominions and of the United

Kingdom without the consent of the majority of the people of Northern Ireland voting in a poll. . . .

Responsible to the new Assembly there was to be an Executive which was to be 'widely acceptable throughout the community'. The legislative and executive powers were carefully defined. The Assembly and Executive were to have no power over Excepted Matters: the Crown, international relations, armed forces, nationality, special powers against terrorism, the police, the appointment and dismissal of judges. Other powers were transferrable to the Executive at the direction of the Secretary of State: until he so transferred them they were to be known as 'reserved matters'. The Act contained a schedule of minimum reserved matters on the day when the new institutions came into force. Simultaneously, the Government pressed on with a reorganisation of local government recommended by a review body headed by Sir Patrick Macrory set up by the Stormont Government in its last days. The setting up of the Housing Executive had been one of the recommendations of this committee: others were the abolition of existing local authorities and the setting up of area boards for education, library, health and personal social services. The remaining functions were to be transferred to twenty-six new District Councils.

Elections to the new District Councils were held in May and to the Assembly in June: the Assembly met for the first time in July. In November, the Secretary of State appointed a power-sharing executive which satisfied the criterion of cross-community support. It was a coalition of Faulkner's Unionists and the SDLP and the Alliance. Faulkner was chief executive and Fitt his deputy; five other Unionists, three members of the SDLP and one of the Alliance completed the Executive, which commanded a clear majority in the Assembly.

In December a tripartite conference was held at Sunningdale in Berkshire between the leaders of the Northern Ireland parties in the new Executive and Ministers of both the United Kingdom and the Republic of Ireland. The purpose was to discuss the Irish dimension: the institutional arrangements laid down in the 1973 Act for consultation and cooperation between North and South. It was agreed to set up a Council of Ireland, with seven ministers from each side forming a Council of Ministers, and a sixty-member Consultative Assembly, elected half by the Dail and half by the Assembly. The Irish Government declared that 'there could be no change in the status of Northern Ireland until a majority of the people of Northern Ireland desired a change in that status'. The Sunningdale agreement was approved in the Assembly by 43 votes to 27. Direct Rule ended on 1 January 1974 and the new Executive took office.

From the start it had to contend with many-sided opposition in Northern Ireland. Republican terrorists stepped up their campaign, fearful that the success of power-sharing would weaken their support among Catholics. Unionists who found power-sharing hard to swallow gagged altogether at the Council of Ireland; the Unionist Party Council rejected Sunningdale and Faulkner had to resign the leadership and found a new party of his own. In Dublin the constitutionality of the Sunningdale agreement was challenged in the courts. Opponents of the agreement claimed that it violated article 2 of the Constitution and the Government defended itself on such narrow technical grounds as to dampen the effect of its acceptance of the status of Northern Ireland.

These difficulties in Ireland were soon overshadowed by wholly extraneous events. The Heath Government, worn down by a British miners' strike, called an election for 28 February. Anti-executive Unionists won only 51 per cent of the Northern Irish vote, but they won 11 of the 12 Westminster seats. Heath's Government was succeeded by a Labour administration under Harold Wilson which proved, in the event, to be less than fully committed to Sunningdale.

In April the three main Unionist parties — the Official Unionist party, the Democratic Unionist party, and William Craig's Vanguard party — formed a United Ulster Unionist Coalition to wage an all-out campaign against both power-sharing and the Council of Ireland. Unionist workers, under Glenn Barr's Ulster Worker's Council, called a general strike, which was supported and enforced by 'Loyalist' paramilitary organisations. When the strike threatened to bring essential services to a standstill, the Unionist members of the Executive resigned, and it fell on 28 May after less than five months in office. Direct Rule had to be resumed, and has continued until the present day.

7.

Direct Rule

Since 1974 successive British governments have made many attempts to secure agreement on a form of devolved administration. In 1974 Merlin Rees brought in the Northern Ireland Act which instituted a Constitutional Convention to consider what provision for government was likely to command the most widespread acceptance. In the elections to the Convention the UUUC won 46 of the 78 seats, and used its majority power to block any proposals for further power-sharing, as advocated by the SDLP. No executive, the Unionists argued, should include those whose attitudes revealed opposition to the very existence of the State. All parties, however, did favour the return of devolved government, and most preferred a unicameral legislature elected by PR. There was general favour for a Bill of Rights and some provision for increased participation by Catholics. But the eventual report favoured a Stormont-type system of parliamentary majority-based cabinet government. The British Government rejected these proposals as lacking cross-community support.

In 1977 the Secretary of State proposed a five-point plan for devolution to the four major parties: these talks were broken off by the Unionists in protest against a statement by the Irish Prime Minister, Jack Lynch. In demanding the withdrawal of the constitutional Guarantee and calling for a phased British withdrawal, Lynch claimed to have received from Wilson a guarantee that there would be no devolution without power-sharing. A further conference on the Government of Northern Ireland was held in 1980 under the chairmanship of Humphrey Atkins, Secretary of State in Mrs Thatcher's first government. It was attended by the DUP, SDLP and Alliance parties, but once again failed to reach any agreement on the fundamental issue of providing for the participation in government of representatives of the Catholic minority.

Meanwhile, under continuing direct rule, the Westminster Government sought for ways of defeating terrorism in Northern Ireland which would not alienate Catholic opinion. In the early seventies some prisoners continued to be detained without trial, others were brought before Diplock courts. The Gardiner Committee, reviewing the emergency laws in 1975, recommended that internment should be completely ended and that all suspects should be dealt with in the special courts; once convicted, they should be treated as ordinary criminals and not given the special status they had enjoyed since Whitelaw's Secretaryship. This policy of 'criminalisation' was adopted: the last internees were released in December 1975 and no one convicted of offences committed after March 1976 has been given special category status.

The ending of internment and the increased use of Diplock courts had consequences which increased rather than diminished Catholic alienation. The difficulties of securing evidence against suspects led to brutal methods of interrogation at Castlereagh in Belfast and in Gough barracks in Armagh. After complaints of beatings and other ill-treatment laid by Amnesty International, the Government appointed the Bennett Inquiry. Its proposals led to strict controls being imposed, and observed, on the conduct of interrogation. But this reform, in its turn, led to an increased reliance on the evidence of accomplices, now that direct confessions were harder to come by. The systematic use of informers, or 'supergrasses', has disquieted both Catholics and Protestants. It has led to many people, both Catholic and Protestant, being convicted and imprisoned as terrorists on the uncorroborated evidence of informers.

When special category status was ended, many members of the IRA convicted in Diplock courts refused to wear prison clothes. When they were denied their own clothes they 'went on the blanket', and later enacted a 'dirty protest' by smearing the walls of their cells with excrement. Failing to win any concessions, a number of prisoners went on hunger strike in 1980 and 1981. Governments in the Republic and Church leaders pleaded with Mrs Thatcher's Government for some flexibility in response to these protests. They attracted Catholic sympathy to such an extent that in 1981 one hunger striker, Bobby Sands, was elected to the Westminster Parliament in a by-election and two other strikers were elected to the Irish Dail. Rioting triggered by the hunger strikes caused more than fifty deaths in 1981, even though the European Commission on Human Rights had found that the sufferings of the protesting prisoners were self-inflicted. The tough policy of Mrs Thatcher's first years was due in part to revulsion against the assassination of popular British figures such as Airey Neave, blown up as he was leaving the House of Commons, and Earl Mountbatten, killed while on holiday in the Republic of Ireland. But undoubtedly the policy helped to polarise the communities and boosted Catholic support for Provisional Sinn Fein, the political counterpart of the Provisional IRA.

It had long been IRA policy to boycott elections and to treat the political process as irrelevant to the main issue of the armed struggle against British occupation. But from the time of the hunger strikes revolutionary Republicans took a much greater interest in political activity and began to run candidates in elections. Sinn Fein did not enter candidates for the Westminster election of May 1979 which put Mrs Thatcher into power, nor in the European elections of the following month, in which Ian Paisley, John Hume, and the Unionist John Taylor were returned to represent Northern Ireland. But after its success in by-elections at the time of the hunger strike, it adopted the joint politico-military strategy summed up in the slogan 'The armalite in one hand, and the ballot in another'. Soon Sinn Fein was given an opportunity to try its fortunes in a province-wide election.

In 1982 Secretary of State James Prior introduced a Bill to enable the Northern Ireland Assembly, and an administration answerable to it, to resume legislative and executive functions. Under the Bill, the Assembly was to have a purely consultative function until legislative powers were devolved to it by Order in Council. Under a system of 'rolling devolution', individual powers could be devolved to the extent to which the Westminster Parliament was satisfied that such an order was likely to command widespread acceptance throughout the community. Elections to the revived Assembly were held in 1982. Fifty-nine per cent of the votes were cast for Unionist parties, the OUP receiving 30 per cent and the DUP 23 per cent. The Alliance party won 9 per cent and other centrist groups 3 per cent. Of the nationalist votes, totalling 31.8 per cent 19 per cent of the vote went to the SDLP and 10 per cent to Sinn Fein.

The Prior Assembly continued in session until 1986 and from time to time exercised a consultative and scrutinising role; but no legislative powers were ever devolved to it, since it had been consistently boycotted by the SDLP and by Sinn Fein, and was temporarily boycotted by the Official Unionists. In the General Election of 1983 the SDLP vote dropped to 18 per cent and Sinn Fein rose to nearly 15 per cent. Constitutional nationalists, North and South, began to fear that in the 1984 European elections Sinn Fein might overtake the SDLP vote and thenceforth claim to be the preferred representatives of the Catholic community.

Direct Rule since 1974 had failed, therefore, to reduce support for the IRA among Catholics. Though terrorist violence had diminished between 1972, when 474 lives had been lost in the province, and 1982, when 95 died, the overall toll taken by the fourteen years of the troubles was horrendous. Between January 1969 and June 1983 2304 people had lost their lives in the province: a loss of lives equivalent, in proportionate terms, to the killing of some 81,000 in Britain. In addition, over 24,000 people had been injured or maimed in over 43,000 separate incidents of shootings, bombings and arson. The majority of deaths were caused by paramilitaries, Catholic or Protestant: Republicans had killed 1264, Loyalists 613. The security forces had caused 264 deaths, and had themselves sustained a loss of 702 lives. The prison population in 1983 was about 2500: the highest figure, in proportion to population size, in the whole of Western Europe. Between 1978 and 1982 more than 22,000 people had been arrested and interrogated: a figure comparable to three-quarters of a million in England.

Northern Ireland was not a uniquely dangerous place: in 1981 the risk of being murdered in the United States was considerably higher than the risk of being killed by terrorists in Northern Ireland, and the chance of meeting a violent death in France, where road deaths are double those in the six counties, was much greater than that in Northern Ireland. But feelings of insecurity, outrage and despair were common among those who, from either community, surveyed the recent history of the province. It was in an attempt to counter these negative responses, and to fill the vacuum left by the failure of British Government initiatives, that the New Ireland Forum was established in 1983.

8.

The New Ireland Forum

When Mrs Thatcher became Prime Minister in May 1979 the Irish Fianna Fail Government was led by Jack Lynch. The two met briefly in September after Earl Mountbatten's funeral. In December Lynch retired, and was succeeded as Taoiseach (Prime Minister) by Charles Haughey. Haughey had been a member of Lynch's Government in 1970 and had been dismissed because of disagreements over policy with regard to Northern Ireland: subsequently he was tried, and acquitted, on a charge of illegal arms importation. As Prime Minister in May and December 1980 he held summit meetings with Mrs Thatcher. In the communiqué following the May meeting he affirmed that it was the wish of the Irish Government to secure the unity of Ireland 'by agreement and in peace', at the same time accepting that 'any change in the constitutional status of Northern Ireland would only come about with the consent of a majority of the people of Northern Ireland'. Both Prime Ministers seemed anxious to inaugurate a new period of co-operation between the British and Irish Governments, and after the December summit a number of joint studies were commissioned, covering possible new institutional structures, citizenship rights, security matters, economic co-operation and measures to encourage mutual understanding, 'in order to assist them in their special consideration of the totality of relationships within the islands'.

By the time these studies were completed, Mr Haughey was no longer in office. The Fianna Fail Government was replaced, in June 1981, by a coalition of the Fine Gael and Labour parties, headed by Garret FitzGerald. Dr FitzGerald, the son of a Presbyterian Unionist mother and a Catholic Republican who had been in the GPO in 1916, had a deep commitment to reconciliation between North and South. No sooner had he become Prime Minister than he announced a 'constitu-

37

tional crusade' to reform the Republic's constitution and purge it, *inter alia*, of elements offensive to Northerners.

The first meeting between FitzGerald and Thatcher took place on 6 November 1981, at Downing Street. They received the reports of the Anglo-Irish joint studies commissioned the year before: all these, except the one on security, were later published. They decided to establish an Anglo-Irish Intergovernmental Council, to give institutional expression to the unique relationship between the two countries and their Governments. This was to involve regular meetings between the two Governments at ministerial and official levels to discuss matters of common concern. It was agreed that it would be for the Parliaments concerned to consider whether there should be an Anglo-Irish body at Parliamentary level comprising members to be drawn from the British and Irish Parliaments, the European Parliament, and any elected Northern Irish body. The two leaders planned to intensify economic co-operation and to extend the privileged treatment which each country offered to citizens of the other in respect of voting rights.

Once again an agreed statement was made on the issue of consent, echoing the words of the Sunningdale and Haughey communiqués:

> The Taoiseach affirmed that it was the wish of the Irish Government and, he believed, of the great majority of the people of the island of Ireland, to secure the unity of Ireland by agreement and in peace. The Prime Minister affirmed, and the Taoiseach agreed, that any change in the constitutional status of Northern Ireland would require the consent of a majority of the people of Northern Ireland. The Prime Minister said that, if that consent were to be expressed as a result of a poll conducted in accordance with the Northern Ireland Constitution Act, 1973, the British Government would of course accept their decision and would support legislation in the British Parliament to give effect to it.

In 1982, between March and December, there was a brief Fianna Fail administration under Haughey before FitzGerald's coalition returned to power. Anglo-Irish relations were placed under strain at this time by the Falklands War: the Irish Government was unwilling to co-operate for long with the sanctions which the European Community imposed upon Argentina. It was not until 1983 that another Anglo-Irish summit took place. But the most important development in 1983 was the setting up of the New Ireland Forum in Dublin.

The Forum arose from an initiative of John Hume, now leader of the SDLP. His idea was that members of the Catholic and nationalist constitutionalist parties should come together to spell out the way in which they hoped to achieve the unity of Ireland by consent, and to protect, in a new Ireland, the identity and interests of Northern Protestants. Thus they would undercut the claim of the paramilitary groups to be the only true exponents of Irish nationalism. In particular, a dramatic initiative by constitutional nationalists might avert the danger that the supporters of Sinn Fein might outvote the SDLP in an election and thus offer a pretext of legitimacy to the 'armed struggle'.

The New Ireland Forum began its deliberations in Dublin Castle on Monday, 30 May and took a year to report. The Chairman of the Forum was the President of University College Galway: of its twenty-seven members, nine were from Fianna Fail, including Mr Haughey and his former Foreign Minister Brian Lenihan, and seven were from Fine Gael, including the Taoiseach, his Foreign Minister Peter Barry, and the constitutional expert John Kelly. Five members represented the Labour party, under the Deputy Prime Minister Dick Spring, and five represented the SDLP, including John Hume, Seamus Mallon and Austin Currie. Eleven public meetings of the Forum between September and February gave an opportunity for oral submissions from various groups, which were later published.

The Forum began with high hopes. In his opening speech Dr FitzGerald said:

> All of the political parties in the New Ireland Forum will in effect for a period of months be sacrificing some of their interests and some of their independence. In deciding to do so, our parties have demonstrated an awareness of the deepening crisis in Northern Ireland and a willingness to put country before party. This is an encouraging augury for the success of our work. By this decision our parties, which are supported by the votes of well over 90 per cent of the nationalist people on this island, demonstrate on behalf of those we represent a powerful collective rejection of murder, bombing and all the other cruelties that are being inflicted on the

population of Northern Ireland in an attempt to secure political change by force. Let the men of violence take note of this unambiguous message from the nationalist people of Ireland: the future of the island will be built by the ballot box, and by the ballot box alone.

Of the public sessions, the most memorable was that of Thursday, 9 February when a delegation of the Irish Episcopal Conference gave evidence. Those who watched the proceedings on television were impressed less by the content of what was said than by the unprecedented novelty, in an Irish context, of bishops being severely cross-examined by politicians. Bishop Cahal Daly of Down and Connor began with a resounding statement.

The Catholic Church in Ireland totally rejects the concept of a confessional state. We have not sought and we do not seek a Catholic state for a Catholic people. We believe that the alliance of Church and State is harmful for the Church and harmful for the state. We rejoiced when the ambiguous formula regarding the special position of the Catholic Church was struck out of the Constitution by the electorate of the Republic.

Politicians from several parties sought to elicit the real substance of this statement. Would this mean that divorce would be allowed in a united Ireland? There could be no diminution, the bishops replied, of the civil and religious rights of the Protestants of Northern Ireland. But consider, Deputy Kelly insisted, the constitution of the present twenty-six-county Republic. Was there not a case for changing that? If divorce would be permitted in a thirty-two-county Republic, why not in a twenty-six-county one? Would the bishops oppose a removal of the constitutional bar against any divorce legislation?

Dr C. Daly: I am afraid, with very great respect, I would feel that that is a political question which is not appropriate for us to answer.

Deputy Kelly: It is not a political question, but I do agree that it is probably the first time since St Patrick arrived that the representatives of the hierarchy were asked to think on their feet.

As the months passed, it became obvious that it was proving difficult to secure agreement between the parties in the Forum. The need to conclude before the European election of June 1984 gave Haughey a chance to insist, as a price of his continued participation, that the Report should go a long way towards endorsing the traditional Fianna Fail support for a United Ireland. Consequently, the document which appeared in May 1984 was uneven, ambiguous and not entirely consistent.

No one could quarrel with the introduction in which the Report affirmed the importance and urgency of its task.

> More than thirty years after European statesmen successfully resolved to set aside their ancient quarrels and to work together in the European Community, the continuation of the conflict in Northern Ireland represents a dangerous source of instability in Western Europe and a challenge to the democratic values which Europe shares in common with North America and the rest of the Western world.

But the Report went on to present a distinctly partisan account of the historical origins of Northern Ireland's troubles. It blamed the problems on the 1920 partition settlement and accused British Governments since 1969 of having no policies other than those of crisis management. The account given in earlier chapters of this book shows that both of these allegations were unfounded. But even more important than the bias in the Forum Report's positive historical account are the factors which it ommitted.

The first neglected point is that the history of the Republic itself is seen by terrorists as legitimising their role. The Provisional IRA does not recognise as legitimate any Dublin Government since 1922, but its members take as their role models the Republicans of 1916 and the Sinn Feiners of 1918–21 who were also acknowledged as founding fathers by some of the parties to the Forum. The combination of the ballot box and the rifle was the combination which led to the establishment of the twenty-six counties as an independent state. All parties to the Forum had forsworn violence and disowned the PIRA; but the common history and common heroes shared by PSF and the Forum parties were no less a part of the historic problem than were the repressive measures taken by British Governments throughout the century.

Moreover, the Forum, while it did not call for British forces to be withdrawn from Northern Ireland, either immediately or at a specified future date, failed to emphasise the real danger of an outbreak of civil war in Northern Ireland if British forces were to withdraw, or if a precipitate political initiative were to alienate Unionist opinion beyond breaking point. Loyalist paramilitaries, too, have role models among the founding fathers of their state: it was the threat of illegal force by Carson's UVF which defeated the Home Rule legislation of 1914. Fears of civil war cannot be dismissed as unrealistic. British withdrawal from the twenty-six counties in 1921 had been followed by civil war between Catholic and Catholic; a British withdrawal from the six counties, following a treaty negotiated with the Dublin Government, might be no less likely to be followed by a more bloody civil war between Catholic and Protestant in Northern Ireland, spilling over into the entire island.

British commentators, however, gave an unequivocal welcome to the Forum's condemnation of the paramilitaries.

The negative effect of IRA violence on British and Unionist attitudes cannot be emphasised enough. Their terrorist acts create anger and indignation and a resolve not to give in to violence under any circumstances. They have the effect of stimulating additional security measures which further alienate the nationalist section of the community. They obscure the underlying political problem. They strengthen Unionist resistance to any form of dialogue and accommodation with nationalists. Similarly, terrorist acts by extreme Loyalist groups which affect innocent nationalist people have a correspondingly negative impact on nationalist attitudes. The involvement of individual members of the security forces in a number of violent crimes has intensified this impact. Every act of murder and violence makes a just solution more difficult to achieve. The greatest threat to the paramilitary organisations would be determined constitutional action to reach and sustain a just and equitable solution and thus to break the vicious circle of violence and repression. No group must be permitted to frustrate by intimidation and threats of violence the implementation of a policy of mutual accommodation.

The fourth chapter of the Forum Report, 'An Assessment of the Present Problem', evaluated current British policies and went on to characterise the identities and attitudes of the Nationalist and Unionist communities. It was the first time an attempt has been made within the context of Irish Nationalism to spell out the positive characteristics of Unionism. In any arrangements for a new Ireland, not only Nationalists but Unionists also must be allowed effective political, symbolic and administrative expression of their identity.

The central chapter of the Forum Report was the fifth, which aimed to spell out the requirements which were the necessary elements of 'a framework within which a new Ireland could emerge'. Since the Irish Prime Minister was later to insist, on many occasions, that this statement of requirements was the kernel of the Forum, it is worth while to reproduce their essentials here.

(1) A fundamental criterion of any new structures and processes must be that they will provide lasting peace and stability.

(2) Attempts from any quarter to impose a particular solution through violence must be rejected along with the proponents of such methods. It must be recognised that the new Ireland which the Forum seeks can come about only through agreement and must have a democratic basis.

(3) Agreement means that the political arrangements for a new and sovereign Ireland would have to be freely negotiated and agreed to by the people of the North and by the people of the South.

(4) The validity of both the Nationalist and Unionist identities in Ireland and the democratic rights of every citizen on this island must be accepted; both of these identities must have equally satisfactory, secure and durable, political administrative and symbolic expression and protection.

(5) Lasting stability can be found only in the context of new structures in which no tradition will be allowed to dominate the other, in which there will be equal rights and opportunities for all, and in which there will be provision for formal and effective guarantees for the protection of individual human rights and of the communal and cultural rights of both Nationalists and Unionists.

(6) Civil and religious liberties and rights must be guaranteed

and there can be no discrimination or preference in laws or administrative practices, on grounds of religious belief or affiliation; government and administration must be sensitive to minority beliefs and attitudes and seek consensus.

(7) New arrangements must provide structures and institutions including security structures with which both Nationalists and Unionists can identify on the basis of political consensus; such arrangements must overcome alienation in Northern Ireland and strengthen stability and security for all the people of Ireland.

(8) New arrangements must ensure the maintenance of economic and social standards and facilitate, where appropriate, integrated economic development, North and South.

(9) The cultural and linguistic diversity of the people of all traditions, North and South, must be preserved and fostered as a source of enrichment and vitality.

(10) Political action is urgently required to halt disillusionment with democratic politics and the slide towards further violence. Britain has a duty to respond *now* in order to ensure that the people of Northern Ireland are not condemned to yet another generation of violence and sterility. The parties in the Forum by their participation in its work have already committed themselves to join in a process directed towards that end.

It was difficult, in general, to disagree with the requirements thus set out. But there were a number of ambiguities. What, exactly, was the 'New Ireland' for which these were prerequisites? Was it simply an Ireland free from violence and discrimination? In that case, no one could fail to be in favour of a New Ireland, and the New Ireland might take many forms, including a continuation of the constitutional *status quo*. On the other hand, when the Report spoke of 'a new and sovereign Ireland' there was a strong innuendo that the new Ireland would take the form of a single sovereign state.

The third of the requirements was ambiguous. It was read by Unionists as meaning that they would have to go into a United Ireland whether they liked it or not; only then would they be consulted about the particular institutions within the new thirty-two-county state. The Irish Prime Minister and his spokesmen interpreted the clause as meaning that no united Ireland would be set up without consent: it should be read as if it ran 'any political arrangements for a new and sovereign Ireland would have to be freely negotiated'. But Mr Haughey explained the paragraph in the same sense as the Unionists. And he should have known what it meant: for it was in fact an echo of a remark in his own opening speech to the first session of the Forum: 'Agreement and consent means that the political arrangements in Ireland to be established following the cessation of the British military and political presence will have to be negotiated, agreed, and consented to by the people of Ireland, North and South, or by their political representatives acting on their behalf.' So the Unionist distaste for requirement three of the Forum Report could not be dismissed as paranoia, however genuine Dr FitzGerald's desire to interpret it as leaving open the question of a united Ireland.

Chapter Five, indeed, went on to conclude that 'a unitary state, achieved by agreement and consent, embracing the whole of Ireland and providing irrevocable guarantees for the protection and preservation of both the Unionist and the Nationalist identities, is the particular structure of political unity which the Forum would wish to see established'. It also put forward a federal/confederal state, and a system of joint authority, as proposals it had received as to 'how Unionist and Nationalist identities and interests could be accommodated in different ways and in varying degrees in a new Ireland'. Finally, it stressed that 'the parties in the Forum remain open to discuss other views which may contribute to political development'. It was this final, open-ended clause which was to be emphasised in succeeding months by Dr FitzGerald. The Forum, he insisted, provided not a blueprint but an agenda.

The sixth, seventh and eighth chapters, however, did spell out, in minimum detail, what was intended by the three options of the unitary state, the federal/confederal system and the proposal of joint authority. In the next chapter we shall examine the practicality of each of these proposals.

9.

Ireland United or Federated?

A unitary state, according to the sixth chapter of the Forum Report, would embrace the island of Ireland governed as a single unit under one Government and one Parliament elected by all the people of the island. 'Such a state would represent a constitutional change of such magnitude as to require a new Constitution that would be non-denominational.' The Constitution, formulated at an all-round constitutional conference convened by the British and Irish Governments, would guarantee civil and religious liberties, and incorporate the clauses of the European Convention on Human Rights, with a right of access to the European Court of Human Rights. No significant obstacle existed to the creation of a unified legal system throughout the island; in a unitary state there would also be a single police service. Unification could be hoped to promote administrative and economic efficiency. The Forum Report had this to say to reassure Protestants about their position in a unitary state:

> Political and administrative arrangements in a unitary state would be devised to ensure that Unionists would not be denied power or influence in a state where Nationalists would be in a majority. For example, provision could be made for weighted majorities in the Parliament in regard to legislation effecting changes in provisions on issues agreed to be fundamental at the establishment of the new state. In the Senate, Unionists could be guaranteed a minimum number of seats. The powers of the Senate could include effective blocking powers in regard to the issues agreed to be fundamental. Mechanisms for ensuring full Northern participation in an integrated Irish civil service would have to be devised.

The educational system would reflect the two main traditions on the

46

island; the Irish language and culture would continue to be fostered by the state.

The proposals were not very fully spelt out, and few of the signatories to the Forum can really have expected them to be taken seriously. All the evidence available to the Forum suggested that in the foreseeable future agreement and consent to a unitary state would be impossible to obtain from a majority of the electors in the North. All the evidence since the Forum, in particular the hostile reaction to the Hillsborough agreement which fell short of the mildest of the Forum's recommendations, has reinforced what was always obvious. In the debate in the House of Commons on the Forum (2 July 1984) James Prior said: 'There is one overriding and abiding reality from which we cannot escape, and that is that consent is simply not forthcoming for any formulation that denies the Unionists their right not only to belong to the United Kingdom but to be apart from the Republic.' The British Labour party is theoretically committed to the unification of Ireland; but in the same debate the Labour spokesman said that such unification could only be brought about by genuine consent, and 'nobody in his right mind would ask the Loyalist parties to come forward today and declare their consent to unification'.

Since all the constitutional parties in Britain and Ireland, North and South, agree that a unitary state can come about only by consent, it is worth considering what incentives the Forum holds out for a Unionist to consent to such a state. There seem to be three incentives offered in the Forum Report.

The first is the offer to reform the Constitution of the Irish Republic and to entrench the rights of all citizens in the reformed Constitution (6.1 and 6.2). British citizenship would remain and an Irish–British Council, with intergovernmental and interparliamentary structures, would provide expression of Unionists' Britishness (6.6).

Secondly, there was the claim that a unitary state would promote administrative and economic efficiency, and enable the pursuit of common interests of North and South, especially in areas such as agriculture, where these diverge from the interests of Great Britain.

Thirdly, it was implied that the introduction of a unitary state would lead to a reduction in the level of violence in Northern Ireland. This was not emphasised in the Report, but it must have been one of the considerations uppermost in the minds of those who drafted it.

None of these factors seriously presents any motive for Unionist conversion 'to a United Ireland. Even if all the Forum's reforms were enacted, after the appropriate referenda in the Republic, it is hard to see how Protestants would be any better off with respect to their civil rights than they are under British government. The secularisation of the Constitution of the Republic and the proposed guarantees of human rights would not give them any advantages which they do not already enjoy. The political arrangements proposed to allow them, as a minority, to take part in the unitary state are arrangements which believers in a United Ireland reject when they are proposed, in the Northern context, as a safeguard for the Catholic minority in a state dominated by Protestants. So too with the British dimension of citizenship, intergovernmental and interparliamentary structures.

Prima facie the strongest of the three arguments is the economic one, and there may well be long-term advantages in operating the whole island as a single economic unit. It is arguable that the Northern Ireland economy has become too dependent on public expenditure and Westminster transfers. There are attractions in a common policy throughout the island in regard to agriculture, the localisation of industry, export marketing, tourism and economic representation to the EEC. But it is not at all clear that such common policies could be developed only within a unitary state.

What is certain is that the short-term economic effects of a British withdrawal from Northern Ireland could well be disastrous. The Forum published a subsidiary report, *A Comparative Description of the Economic Structure and Situation, North and South*. According to this report, the British subvention to the Northern Exchequer in 1982–3 was £1312 million sterling. According to the same report, living standards in the North, even during the present difficult times, were slightly higher than those in the South (sections 4.1 and 4.5). The report says:

> In 1982–3 the subvention represented about 29 per cent of the North's GDP and 13.8 per cent of that of the South. In the same year the subvention was equivalent to 69 per cent of public levied

revenue raised in the North. Thus the North's dependence on the subvention is such that had it been necessary to replace the subvention in that year by taxes raised in the North it would have required an increase in tax revenue of approximately 69 per cent. Again, in the same year, the subvention amounted to about 29 per cent of public revenue raised in the South. (8.12)

It follows, therefore, from the Forum's own findings that in a united Ireland either citizens of the Republic would have to accept an enormously higher tax burden to afford Northerners a standard of living higher than they enjoy themselves or Northerners must accept a drop in standards of living in addition to renouncing their political aspirations; or Britain would have to continue a massive subvention to a province for which it no longer had any responsibility; or substantial funding would have to be found from some foreign power or international source.

The framers of the Forum Report were well-advised not to stress any dividends to peace and tranquillity which they may have hoped for from a unitary state. For the reunion of Ireland does not hold out a serious hope of the cessation of violence. On the one hand, the setting up of a unitary state would not guarantee the end of IRA violence: nationalist paramilitaries do not recognise the legitimacy of the Southern Government, and once the British had left the North, they might well turn to the task of making a state to their liking in the South. On the Protestant side, there is an even greater likelihood of paramilitary violence: it is already threatened in response to the much more modest Hillsborough proposals. Even if the majority of Unionists were somehow to be persuaded to enter a unitary state, a disaffected minority of them might well take to arms. Since the Protestant community in the North is nearly twice the size of the Catholic community, the minority of them disaffected enough to take up arms might well be twice as large and twice as dangerous as the existing PIRA and INLA.

It is hard, then, to see how self-interest would lead Unionists into a unitary state. But if not self-interest, is there some moral or legal obligation which should oblige them reluctantly to accept it? No doubt deceptions and unfairnesses of various kinds contributed to the drawing of the border, but these were the acts of men long dead, and the border has long been recognised in international law. At the present time the objection to partition is that it goes counter to the aspirations of Irish nationalists: but it is not obvious how much weight, in political matters, should be attached to aspirations. The aspirations of citizens in the Republic of Ireland to incorporate the area of Northern Ireland in their state certainly cannot outweigh the aspirations of the majority of those in the North not to be united. The aspirations of Catholics in the North itself are obviously more important than those of Catholics in the South. If their aspirations could be realised by a redrawing of the border, their claim for this would be a strong one. But in fact hardly any Catholic in the North wishes to see the border redrawn. Since it would be difficult, without huge transfers of population, to devise a practicable revision, most Catholics either want the border to disappear or to stay where it is. In so far as Catholics in the North have aspirations to move Northern Ireland as a whole into the Irish Republic, these aspirations cannot outweigh the contrary aspirations of the Protestant majority. In so far as they are aspirations to have a due share in the running of Northern Ireland as it now exists, these aspirations constitute a strong moral claim, but one which of its nature is to be satisfied in some other way than by a unitary state.

Of course, Catholics in the North have a legitimate claim to have their cultural identity respected and maintained. Many Northern Catholics wish also to have political involvement in the Republic of Ireland; for instance, by voting and standing for election. In fact, Northern Catholics have been active in Southern politics, through membership of the Irish Senate. Only rather slight amendments to the existing citizenship laws of the United Kingdom and of the Republic would enable Northern Catholics, if they wished, to take a full part in the political life of both states. Aspirations of this kind, therefore, can be achieved under British sovereignty and do not require for their fulfilment a unitary state.

The seventh chapter of the Forum Report sketched models of a federal or confederal arrangement for the Government of Ireland. Each state, North and South, would have its own Parliament and Executive. The Central Government would have authority for security. In a federal arrangement, there would be a Federal Parliament with one or two chambers. Laws relating to previously agreed fundamental issues could be passed only if they received the support of a weighted majority of the legislature. Various arrangements for the division of powers between the Central and State Governments could be envisaged: perhaps agriculture, industry, energy, transport, industrial promotion and marketing might be more efficiently administered at federal level, while education, health, housing and social welfare might be best administered by the individual states. A President could be appointed alternately from the Northern and Southern states.

A confederal model also might be devised, differing from a federal model in that less power would be concentrated at the centre. In a federation, certain powers are vested in individual states, while residual power resides with the Federal Government. In a confederal system, the powers at the centre are specified, while residual power remains with the states. The powers held at the centre, the Forum Report suggested, might be restricted to foreign policy, external and internal security, and perhaps currency and monetary policy. Unionists would have powers, in the Northern Parliament, which could not be removed by the Southern Parliament; they would have parallel British citizenship and could maintain special links with Britain.

Others besides the drafters of the Forum Report have seen attractions in a confederal arrangement for the Btitish Isles. Had the proposals contained in the Kilbrandon Commission on the Constitution been accepted, a confederation of England, Scotland, Wales, and the two parts of Ireland, within the European Community and perhaps also within the Commonwealth, might have seemed an attractive possibility. A confederation consisting simply of the two parts of Ireland is a much less promising prospect. Unionist consent to leave the United Kingdom would be a prerequisite, and that is likely to be given only with the most extreme reluctance. In particular, Unionists are likely to be totally unwilling to accept an arrangement which would mean that the responsibility for internal security passed away from Westminster and Belfast into the hands of a central government dominated by Irishmen from the South. Foreign policy and external security also present problems, since Ireland is committed to a policy of neutrality, while Northern Ireland, as part of the United Kingdom, is as firmly committed to NATO, and is unlikely to wish to change this commitment. As with the prospect of a united Ireland, it is difficult to see what incentive the Forum Report holds out to Unionists to wish to separate themselves from the United Kingdom and enter a federation or confederation with the Republic.

10.
Joint Authority

The most original proposal in the Forum Report was a model of joint authority to accommodate Nationalist and Unionist identities and interests in Northern Ireland. The eighth chapter says:

> Under joint authority, the London and Dublin governments would have equal responsibility for all aspects of the government of Northern Ireland.

A proposal for joint sovereignty had been made in a submission to the New Ireland Forum in November 1983 by Dr Bernard Cullen, from the Queen's University of Belfast, from a Unionist background, and Dr Richard Kearney of University College Dublin, from a Nationalist background. Having described the ethos and aspirations of the two communities, they went on to say:

> Both communities must renounce the absolute separatism of what we have called their 'ultimate aspirations' [namely, separatism from Ireland and Britain, respectively]. They can do this, however, without sacrificing the national identity which they see as guaranteeing their cultural security. In each case, the kernel of their legitimate aspiration is retained, but in a modified form. The Unionists demand British sovereignty over N.I. The Nationalists demand Irish sovereignty over N.I. It is in the light of the foregoing arguments that we are proposing joint British and Irish sovereignty over N.I.

The authors sketched out what this would involve: either a British or Irish passport could be carried, there would be two national anthems and national flags; religious views of one particular denomination could not be enshrined in law, whether they concerned sexual ethics or sabbath observance. Northern Ireland would have a devolved Parliament and Government, subject to an intergovernmental commission, and the citizens of the province would send representatives to the Dail and to Westminster.

The Joint Authority proposal in the Forum Report avoided tackling the issue of sovereignty: but many readers felt that the proposal amounted to joint sovereignty in all but name. In the Report itself only a broad concept of joint authority was outlined, but a subcommittee of the Forum worked out the idea in detail and listed its advantages and disadvantages. The Forum presumably made use of the Report in its deliberations, but did not publish it. However, the subcommittee's Report was published unofficially in the *Irish Times* of 9 May 1984. According to its first paragraph:

> Joint authority is the equal sharing of responsibility and authority for all aspects of the government of Northern Ireland by the governments of Great Britain and Ireland. Power over all matters relating to Northern Ireland would be vested in and exercised by an Executive Joint Authority of the two governments. This Executive Joint Authority would appoint a Joint Authority Commission to run Northern Ireland. Beneath this there could be whatever levels of local responsibility that the Executive Joint Authority might wish to establish and were agreed to by local representatives. A binding agreement or treaty between the two governments would establish the Executive Joint Authority.

Joint authority, the subcommittee felt, provided the essential element of joint sovereignty — namely, responsibility for all aspects of government and international relations — while avoiding, unlike joint sovereignty, any clash with articles 2 and 3 of the Irish Constitution. It might, however, be necessary to enact an amendment to the Constitution to the following effect: 'No provision of this Constitution invalidates laws enacted, acts done, or measures adopted by the State necessitated by the Agreement/Treaty on Joint Authority in regard to Northern Ireland entered into by the Irish Government.' Simultaneously with the introduction of joint authority, a Bill of Rights should be enacted and a Constitutional Court set up to interpret and enforce the Treaty.

The Report envisaged two models of joint authority. One was a system of 'shared direct rule' in which the Joint Authority Commission exercised all executive powers; the other was a system in which certain powers were reserved to the Commission while the main executive authority was exercised by a local executive supported by a locally elected Assembly. In the second model the Assembly could have the powers to be 'transferred' under the 1973 Act: housing, physical infrastructure, agriculture, education, commerce, minor taxation, health and social services. However, either of the two Commissioners appointed by the British and Irish Governments would have a veto on legislation or action by the Assembly. An Executive would be formed from the Assembly: the Report left open the question whether it should be chosen by majority rule (weighted or unweighted) or along the lines of power-sharing or rolling devolution. If the Executive became deadlocked, or collapsed, transferred powers would return to the Joint Authority Commission.

The subcommittee recommended that joint responsibility for internal security and for a criminal justice regime should be a central component of joint authority, and it attached importance to 'the immediate establishment of a new police force based on secondment from existing police forces in Great Britain and Ireland with a new command structure'. If this were representative of the whole community, and sufficiently large and well-equipped, it should remove the necessity for the permanent presence of a military back-up.

The Treaty was to provide for full recognition and symbolic expression of British and Irish identities: all citizens would have joint citizenship rights; the flags of both states should have equal status; Northern Ireland citizens could use passports and consuls of either jurisdiction.

Turning to economic arrangements, the subcommittee proposed that existing tax levels within Northern Ireland would continue to apply. The overall level of public expenditure would be determined by the Executive Joint Authority; the shortfall between revenue and expenditure, which is now borne by Westminster, would be borne by the two states jointly, in proportions to be negotiated.

The subcommittee concluded with a sober account of the advantages and disadvantages to be expected from the institution of joint authority. The pros and cons were considered from several points of view; as an example of the subcommittee's effort to strike a fair balance, we may quote the treatment of likely Unionist reaction. On the advantage side, it was said (sections 39–40):

> The likely opposition of Unionists might fall short of alienation, or sustained widespread violent reaction, since their Britishness, Protestantism, living standards and security would be upheld, with the continued involvement of Britain. If both Governments were fully committed it would not be possible for Unionists or Nationalists to block implementation of the basic necessary structures. . . . There need be no weak link, exposed to pressures (such as the vulnerability of the Faulkner Unionists to the Loyalist strike in 1974). If any subordinate structures collapsed, the joint authorities could simply carry on joint direct rule.

On the other hand, among the disadvantages was listed (section 48):

> Unionists might not identify with structures which went beyond the Sunningdale arrangements against which they had reacted strongly. Unionists are already disenchanted with direct rule by English overlords: they could be even less enthusiastic about a form of double direct rule. An absence of identification with the structures could promote greater instability than already exists.

The most interesting and original section of the Report considered what should happen if and when Nationalists became a majority in Northern Ireland. Perhaps the British would wish to end their involvement in accordance with section 1 of the 1973 Act; and indeed Nationalists might hope that joint authority might gradually win Unionist confidence and lessen Unionist repugnance to Irish unity.

> On the other hand, the British might wish to remain involved even after that point was reached, or might feel obliged to respond to a Unionist wish that they should. It could be argued that if Joint Authority is justified where there is a Nationalist minority of 35–40% it would be equally justified where there was a substantial Unionist minority in the North.

The subcommittee's Report shows a greater sensitivity to the true position of Unionists than do any of the published parts of the Forum. But even this Report greatly underestimated the likely extent of Unionist resentment at the proposals it contained. Joint authority of such an all-embracing kind was joint sovereignty in all but name. Such a significant alteration in the sovereignty of Northern Ireland could not be made without the consent of a majority of the population, and that consent was unlikely to be given to such an extensive involvement of the Irish Government in every detail of the province's internal and external affairs.

It is true that the exact terms of the guarantee in section 1 of the Northern Ireland Constitution Act 1973 stated only that 'in no event will Northern Ireland or any part of it cease to be part of Her Majesty's dominions and of the United Kingdom without the consent of the majority'; it does not expressly rule out that, while continuing to be part of the United Kingdom, the province should also become part of the Republic of Ireland. But to set up an executive joint authority by binding treaty would undoubtedly be against the spirit of the guarantee which was intended to recognise what Mr Prior, in the debate on the Forum, called 'The Unionists' right . . . not only to belong to the United Kingdom *but to be apart from the Republic'*.

But though the Report's proposals stood little chance of implementation as they stood, the preparation of the Report was a significant event. It was valuable to have the practical implications of joint authority spelt out so clearly and fairly. Others were led by reading the Report to reflect on forms of joint authority which were more clearly distinct from joint sovereignty: versions, for instance, in which foreign policy and defence matters would remain the exclusive responsibility of the UK Government. Most significant of all was the fact that these proposals for joint government of Northern Ireland had been made at all within the Nationalist framework of the Forum. As one Westminster politician put it, 'For decades Nationalists have been saying "Brits out" — but joint authority is by definition "Brits in".' It was a remarkable development that the framers of the Report were happy to recommend that the Union Jack should continue to fly over Belfast even after the long-awaited, millennial, day on which Catholics began to outnumber Protestants in Northern Ireland.

11.

Blackballs and Blueprints

In Northern Ireland both Unionist parties reacted to the New Ireland Forum. Each of them produced both a positive and a negative document in response. The Official Unionists pre-empted the Forum Report with their own proposals, contained in the paper 'The Way Forward' published in April 1984. They followed this up with a critique of the Forum Report in November, written by Peter Smith, under the title 'Opportunity Lost'. The Democratic Unionists responded to the Forum in the reverse order: first appeared a savagely critical paper. 'The Unionist Case: The Forum Report Answered', by Jim Allister, Nigel Dodds and Sam Wilson; later came the more constructive document, 'Ulster the Future Assured', by Jim Allister, William Beattie, Ivan Foster and Peter Robinson. The two positive papers were presented to the Northern Ireland Assembly Report Committee on Devolution. This body had started work in June 1984 with the task of examining 'how the Assembly might be strengthened and progress made towards legislative and executive devolution'. The two Unionist papers were published as part of the Committee's second report, along with an Alliance party paper, on 19 February 1985.

The two negative papers contained a number of criticisms of the New Ireland Forum report which were substantially justified. The report is ambiguous on the role of consent, it is tendentious in its account of the past, unrealistic in its proposals for the future. Each paper devoted considerable space to documenting what it regarded as the disastrous influence of the Roman Catholic Church on political process in the South of Ireland. Each paper was particularly severe on the proposal for joint authority. We may quote the judgement of 'Opportunity Lost' on this scheme:

It is in the provocative nature of the introduction of joint authority that the real danger lies. Unionists would see it as a first step to a united Ireland. The sight of Irish policemen on Northern Irish streets would inevitably produce a tremendous reaction. The direct involvement of Irish officials in governing Northern Ireland would be a source of great resentment. The tensions thus created would be readily exploited by terrorist organisations on both sides of the divide in Northern Ireland and the joint authority government would then be faced with trouble on two fronts which it could not conceivably cope with.

It is a measure of the Forum's lack of understanding of Northern Unionism and, therefore, a clear demonstration of the way in which it tackled its task, that it could put forward such a nonsensical 'solution' to the problem. It is simply unbelievable that any serious student of Northern Ireland could imagine that such an idiotic scheme could work.

The Democratic Unionist paper also attacks joint authority, though it insists on referring to it throughout as joint sovereignty. The tone of its criticism can be judged by listing the subheadings to the paragraphs: 'Joint Sovereignty: its Republican Pedigree and Purpose', 'Joint Sovereignty — A Unconstitutional End to British Ulster', 'Joint Sovereignty — A Stepping Stone to Full Dublin Rule', 'Joint Sovereignty — A Denial of Self-Determination and a Travesty of Democracy', 'Joint Sovereignty — A Mockery of "Consent" and a Practice of Deceit', 'Joint Sovereignty — A Surrender to Terrorism'. 'Indeed', says the paper,

> some would even take the Ulster Unionist to be such a fool as to expect him to believe that Joint Sovereignty would strengthen the British guarantee to Northern Ireland by adding to it the 'guarantee' of the Republic of Ireland that the British connection will continue. This is a palpable lie and deceit. Joint Sovereignty unalterably reverses Northern Ireland's constitutional affiliation as part of the United Kingdom and delivers it out of the United Kingdom irretrievably half-way to an all-Ireland Republic; and all this without the least consent of the people of Northern Ireland.

It is hard to imagine to whom the DUP paper was addressed, and hard to believe that it converted a single person who did not already share its views. Legitimate criticisms of the serious defects in the Forum Report were altogether overlaid by rhetorical abuse, one-sided history and unconcealed bigotry. But some of its comments are worth bearing in mind. One was entitled 'The Green Herring' and read:

> The assumption by some, including, from time to time, Dr Garrett Fitzgerald, that it is the current Constitution of the Republic which keeps Northern Ireland from embracing the concept of Irish unification, is patently false. This is amply demonstrated by the fact that the present Constitution, which dates only from 1937, was not in existence when, in 1921, Northern Ireland opted not to join with the Irish Free State in breaking away from the United Kingdom. So, clearly, it is not the Republic's Constitution — wholly objectionable as it is — which causes Ulster to be determined to remain British.

The Official Unionist riposte to the Forum was a more measured document. But it too suffered from the defect that bedevils so much political argument in Northern Ireland on both sides of the divide: it focused entirely on the unacceptable elements of the other side's position, and made no attempt to measure how far the Forum Report was a genuine offer of new compromise, a genuine advance on previous nationalist dogma. The best it could say of the Forum was this:

> While the Forum Report may reveal a higher degree of understanding of the Unionist position than Irish nationalists have cared to reveal in the past, it still remains woefully inadequate.

'Opportunity Lost' offers an analysis of the motives of the parties to the New Ireland Forum. The Coalition Government 'is terrified of Sinn Fein overspilling out of Northern Ireland into the Republic, igniting the tinder of unemployed youth and the socially deprived, leading to a collapse of the state'. The SDLP 'believes itself to be close to being outflanked by Sinn Fein in Northern Ireland . . . it seeks early action on Irish unity in order to restore its prestige with its electorate'. Altogether, the Unionists claim, 'Sinn Fein, PIRA and INLA represent a greater threat to the Republic, the legitimacy of which these organisations reject, than to Northern Ireland.'

There is an important truth here, however unsympathetically stated. Republican paramilitaries present a problem to the Republic of Ireland no less than to Northern Ireland. What is astonishing is that there should be no sign that the Unionists welcome the realisation of this fact by the authorities of the Republic. It might have been thought that they would be delighted to see Nationalists in the South recognising that they and the Unionists in the North had a common enemy in Sinn Fein. Let us suppose that the Unionist analysis of the Nationalist parties' motives is correct: the Forum aims to prevent a Sinn Fein takeover of the Catholic representation in the North, and a destabilisation of the Government in the Republic. Are these not aims which the Unionists might be expected to applaud? They admit that 'whatever its faults the Irish Republic as presently constituted is infinitely preferable to any creation of a triumphalist Sinn Fein'. Would it not, then, be sensible to hold out a helping hand — however cautiously — to the efforts of the Forum, to prevent a Sinn Fein triumph, North or South? 'Opportunity Lost' complains, with some justice, of the inadequate self-criticism in the Forum Report. But its remarks in this context could be applied with even greater justice to itself:

> The Forum Report illustrates an unhealthy facet of Irish politics. This is the tendency for politicians to blame their misfortunes on their opponents, rather than facing up to the question of whether those misfortunes may not have resulted from their own short-comings (p.9).

The positive Unionist papers, 'The Way Forward' and 'The Future Assured', make less depressing reading. The proposals of the Official Unionists were modest, and deliberately so: but they would have meant, if accepted, a significant move away from direct rule towards local participation in government. The paper accepted that major devolution was blocked by the minority's refusal to consent to majority rule and the majority's refusal to countenance compulsory power-sharing. It proposed, however, that the existing Assembly, while shorn of legislative functions, should become an administrative body for Northern Ireland. The Macrory Report of 1970 had abolished County and County Borough Councils, and recommended that the Stormont Parliament should take over as a Regional Authority. But with the abolition of Stormont a gap was left at the top level of local government: even those functions which were delegated to Area Boards (e.g. Health and Education) were controlled by nominated and not elected bodies. The Official Unionists now proposed that the major regional services should be devolved to the Assembly. There would be no cabinet; instead, the areas of devolved power would be divided among committees. This should encourage minority participation. 'The absence of any party with an overall majority in the foreseeable future would necessitate those compromises and bargains between participating parties which are the essence of real politics.'

In order to safeguard the minority, the document proposes that the Westminster legislation devolving authority should contain a Bill of Rights, and should reserve to itself the power to amend the Bill. Any act of a devolved institution conflicting with a listed right would be voidable. The list of rights should be based on the European Convention, but might need adaptation in the light of the special circumstances of Northern Ireland. The OUP remained 'resolutely opposed to an Irish dimension in the form of a constitutional institution', but 'would not object to an Irish dimension in the form of state recognition of the legitimacy of the fostering of distinctively Irish cultural activities in Northern Ireland, nor to state funding of such activities in proportion to the degree of public participation in them'.

The party stressed that 'The Way Forward' was not meant to be definitive, but was open to negotiation. It insisted, however, that problems were best solved within a Northern Ireland context. It called on the two communities for 'a mutual recognition of each others' hopes and fears. Only rights can be guaranteed, not aspirations, but it is the responsibility of the majority to persuade the minority that the Province is also theirs.'

The Democratic Unionists proposed a more substantial form of devolved government. It set out its framework for democracy thus:

> Democracy has in the past been defined by the leader of the S.D.L.P. as rule by the majority with the consent of the community as a whole. Power-sharing, however, does not meet Mr Hume's criterion, for power-sharing is based on the principle of preventing, or at least inhibiting, in some way the majority from

ruling, with or without the consent of the minority. The D.U.P. proposals, however, ensure that the majority does rule yet at the same time giving a meaningful role, and laying down safeguards, for minorities, regardless of which party or parties form the majority or minority.

The proposals called for a Cabinet system of Government formed by the leader of the largest party or group of parties, which would be responsible to the Assembly. The Assembly would have legislative powers in respect of all transferred matters, and an advisory and monitoring role on non-transferred matters such as security and external relations. There would be departmental committees of eight, with the duty of monitoring each of the government departments: perhaps membership and chairmanships of these committees could be drawn equally from Government and Opposition. To safeguard minorities, if a Bill was rejected by a departmental committee, it would then require a weighted majority of 60 per cent of those voting in the Assembly. A minority — perhaps 30 per cent of the Assembly — could be entitled to require the Secretary of State to refer to the Judicial Committee of the Privy Council any proposed legislation that might be thought discriminatory on grounds of religious or political opinion. The DUP, like the OUP, would be prepared to accept a Northern Ireland Bill of Rights, while it would prefer a Bill for the whole United Kingdom. The DUP recognised that while it opposed power-sharing, the electorate might return a majority of parties committed to the concept. In that case, the DUP would be in opposition.

On the Irish dimension, the document said: 'While the people of Northern Ireland emphatically reject any institutionalised association or other constitutional relationship with the Republic of Ireland, they have no desire to live in hostility with their neighbours in the Republic of Ireland.' There were many areas where co-operation between North and South might be mutually beneficial, but any arrangements to this effect must be made by the Northern Ireland people in Assembly. Any new initiatives North–South must therefore be subsequent to, and not a part of, the establishment of new political institutions in Northern Ireland.

The Alliance party, the third of the parties taking seats in the

Assembly, was smaller than either of the Unionist parties: Alliance members held ten seats to the OUP's twenty-six and the DUP's twenty-one. The party submitted its proposals for devolution on 25 June 1984. The essence of its scheme was a committee system of partnership government based upon the principle of proportionality, the creation of a political right of appeal, and the enactment of a Northern Ireland Bill of Rights.

The committee system of Government would function as follows. The Assembly would have legislative powers. It would elect, by alternative vote, a Chief Executive. It would elect committees in such a way as to reflect the political make-up of the Assembly as decided by the electorate. The chairmen of the committees would also be elected proportionally by the Assembly as a whole, on the system of single transferable vote. Each chairman would have executive responsibility for the day-to-day running of a department, subject to general policy guidelines. First, the chairmen would be elected as a panel, and then the departments allocated. The chairmen of committees would form a finance committee, chaired by the Chief Executive, to allocate resources.

Such a system would ensure a degree of power-sharing, and thus help safeguard minority interests. The Alliance party would also provide a political right of appeal to Westminster at the petition of one-third plus one of the Assembly. Subject to Parliamentary approval, the Secretary of State could prohibit, or annul, Assembly legislation, and to resume partial responsibility for the devolved subject in question.

The Alliance party, even more than the other two parties, favoured a Bill of Rights. It recorded its dissatisfaction with the remedies available for discriminatory actions by public authorities under the 1973 Act, and proposed that the European Code of Human Rights should be incorporated into the law of Northern Ireland without waiting for its incorporation into the law of the United Kingdom as a whole. A Human Rights Commission might take over the functions of the existing Fair Employment Agency, Equal Opportunities Commission, and Standing Advisory Commission on Human Rights.

The Alliance party's response to the New Ireland Forum was guarded. It was in favour of increased co-operation with the Republic and the development of the 'Anglo-Irish process'. But it was opposed to any institutionalised role for the Republic in the political affairs of Northern

Ireland such as proposed by each of the Forum's options, including joint authority.

12.

The Way from the Forum

The reactions of the British mainland parties to the Forum were expressed in a debate in the House of Commons on 2 July 1984. James Prior, in one of his last appearances as Secretary of State, welcomed the positive tone and openness of both the Forum Report and 'The Way Forward'. While warning that political progress was no guarantee of an end to terrorism, and might even in the short run increase it, he expressed the belief that 'the dangers for the people of Northern Ireland of sitting back and doing nothing are greater than the obvious risks of seeking to make some political advance'.

In response to the 'Realities and Requirements' of the Forum, he listed five realities of his own which called for recognition.

First, the reality of Unionist opposition: in so far as any of the Forum models significantly altered the sovereignty of Northern Ireland, it was a dangerous fallacy to expect Unionists to agree to them.

Secondly, Northern Ireland was part of the United Kingdom and internationally recognised as such. This is set out in the 1973 Act, but with or without the Act the consent of the people, freely given, would be necessary for any amendment of the constitutional position.

Thirdly, while Northern Ireland remained in the United Kingdom its government was ultimately a matter for the Westminster Parliament.

The fourth reality was that the needs of the people of Northern Ireland would best be met by a devolved administration which has the support of both sides of the community. 'When it comes to the government and administration of Northern Ireland within the United Kingdom there is no Unionist veto.'

Fifthly, geography, as well as the sentiments of Northern nationalists, called for a close relationship between the United

Kingdom Government and the Republic; perhaps involving, if the Dail and the Westminster Parliaments wished, an interparliamentary body.

He concluded with the hope that discussions between the parties in Northern Ireland (following the proposals in the Assembly's Report Committee) and between the two Governments (following from the Forum) might lead to new progress. 'Unionists can take part in the knowledge that the position of Northern Ireland as part of the United Kingdom is secure. Nationalists can do so knowing that we want to find an acceptable way to involve them and that we are concerned about the views that the Irish government have expressed on their behalf.'

Not all Conservatives took a similarly positive view of the Forum Report. Sir John Biggs-Davison, while praising its tone ('By the standards of Irish and Anglo-Irish political controversy, it is emollient. It is possible to read good will, at least between the lines'), regarded all its proposals as impractical, and found impudent the implication that the abandonment of Northern Ireland should be financed by the British taxpayer. Mr Ivor Stanbrook was more outspoken. The report was 'a humbug, a deceit, a snare, and a delusion'; its objective was 'to expand the frontiers of the Irish Republic'.

The official policy of the Labour party for Ireland was 'unification by consent'. The front bench spokesman, Peter Archer, having said that 'The Opposition believe that the interests of the people of Northern Ireland will be best served by the unification of Ireland' emphasised the necessity for consent with such vigour that a United Ireland disappeared over the distant horizon. It was not so in the speeches from the Labour back benches. Joan Maynard said: 'I do not believe that there will be peace or a solution to the problem until we set a date for Britain's withdrawal from Northern Ireland.' Clare Short claimed that opinion polls showed that the majority of voters in Great Britain wished to withdraw from Northern Ireland. Only withdrawal in the context of the reunification of Ireland could bring about a political solution. Clive Soley, while claiming that many even on the Conservative benches would dearly love the Unionists to consent to a united Ireland, thought that if the British withdrew or even stated a date for withdrawal, that would lead not to a united Ireland but to greater paramilitary activity and probably a smaller independent Northern Ireland.

Mr Soley supported one of the Forum's proposals: police should be recruited and trained on either side of the border as the two Governments think appropriate. Even from the Conservative benches there was some support for the joint authority option: Mr Benyon found it strongly attractive and hoped it would bring a combined police authority, all-Ireland courts, and a revised devolved constitution for the province. He urged the 'leaders of exceptional ability' in London and Dublin to seize on an unparalleled opportunity for political progress.

The leaders of the Northern Irish parties made their positions clear. Mr Molyneaux spelt out the OUP proposals from 'The Way Forward'. He explained to members that there was a difference between the English and the Irish meaning of the word 'consent'. When the Labour party spoke of Unionist consent to a change of sovereignty, they meant 'the free, cheerful, and, to coin a phrase, full-hearted consent of the Ulster people'. Mr Haughey, however, interpreted consent as agreement resulting from pressure and coercion, constitutional and economic. The Forum parties must be convinced that 'free consent will not be achieved in their lifetime and that forced consent is repugnant to the British people'.

The most effective oratory was in the speech of John Hume, who introduced himself as a 'proud author' of the Forum Report. He began recalling the day of the European election in Northern Ireland.

> On that day, around the close of poll, I was in my house in Derry when I heard a commotion in the street. I looked out of the window and saw a group of youths in masks filling bottles with petrol. I was not sure whether, in the heat and emotion at the end of election day, the target was my home or a passing military vehicle. Such occurrences are not unusual in front of my house.
>
> There are 650 members in the House. If I ventured to ask them what they would do in such circumstances, 649 of them would tell me that they would pick up the telephone and ring the police. I did not do that. I knew that had I done so I would simply have made a bad situation worse. That is a stark reality of life in areas of Northern Ireland that do not give their allegiance to the Union.

The moral of the story was simple. Any security policy or system of order must be based on political consensus. Community backing for the forces of law and order was possible only if the community gave its loyalty to the institutions of the state. The Forum was attempting to create the political situation to allow that.

If Unionists had been able to claim that the Forum Report was insufficiently critical of the nationalist tradition, the same complaint could not have been made of Mr Hume's speech.

I do not claim that everybody in the nationalist tradition is all virtue and that everybody else is to blame. We have only to look at our past approach to recognise the mistakes. We have only to look at the narrowness of Irish nationalism, its definition, its sectionalism, and its exclusionism, tied solely to the Gaelic and Catholic traditions and exclusive of other traditions represented in the House from Northern Ireland, to recognise that the narrowness is of itself divisive. It is pushed to its extremes by those who tell us that the height of Irish patriotism is the right not only to die for it but to kill fellow Irishmen for it as well.

There were few surprises in the Rev. Ian Paisley's speech. 'The view that I put before the House today has been massively mandated by the people of Northern Ireland. . . . The elected representatives of Northern Ireland must have some voice in security matters. . . . I do not want to live under any system that is dominated by Roman Catholic social dogma.' He rejected the Forum Report *in toto*:

What does the document hold out? It holds out a unitary state and joint sovereignty or some sort of confederation which would take Northern Ireland out of the United Kingdom and put it into some all-Ireland settlement. That is anathema to the people who sent me to the House. They want no part or lot in it, and they will not have it.

There was one passage, however, in Mr Paisley's speech which must have moved his hearers no less than Mr Hume's account of his own experience.

There is a lobby for peace among the vast majority of people in Northern Ireland. Why should there not be a lobby? I have followed too many funeral processions, I have held too many widows' hands and I have patted too many orphans' heads not to know the agony my people have gone through. They are not only Protestant but Roman Catholic bereaved ones. I have received a lot of stick from Unionists for even going to their homes.

I know what I am talking about. There is a desire for peace. That peace can come only within Northern Ireland. It is up to the elected representatives of the Northern Ireland people to get together and seek a way forward out of this impasse. I am prepared to talk to the elected representatives of the people of Northern Ireland and to try to find some way whereby we can bring hope for a future when there will be something for our kids and young ones growing up, and some sort of political and economic stability. I say that not because I need to say it but because it comes from my heart.

It was not only MPs from Northern Ireland who were made familiar with bereavement in the summer of 1984. Patrick Magee, of the Provisional IRA, planted a bomb in the Grand Hotel Brighton, which exploded during the Conservative party's annual conference. The Prime Minister and other members of the Government narrowly escaped death, five people were killed in their beds, and others seriously injured.

13.
The Kilbrandon Report

Outside Parliament, the most detailed British response to the New Ireland Forum and the Unionist documents came from the Kilbrandon Committee. This was an unofficial group of inquirers, assembled by Lord Kilbrandon at the request of the British Irish Association, to examine the practicability of the Forum and the Unionist proposals. The Committee contained several academics, a journalist, a solicitor, a businesswoman, and politicians of the main parties, including a former Conservative Cabinet Minister, David Howell, and the Deputy Leader of the Opposition in the Lords, Lord Underhill. It began its delibera-tions in May, and after nine plenary meetings and many visits to Ireland, North and South, by smaller groups it reported on 1 November.

The Committee's report analysed and commented on the Forum Report and the Unionist documents. It criticised the one-sided his-torical account in the Forum Report, while broadly agreeing with the Report's assessment of the realities and requirements in Northern Ireland. It regarded as impracticable each of the three frameworks put forward in the Report: unitary state, federal or confederal system, and joint authority. But it considered that the Forum's proposals on joint authority contained ideas which provided scope for progress in North-ern Ireland.

The Committee unanimously recommended a number of specific measures which it thought would offer reassurance to the minority that their aspirations were taken seriously, while being capable, in an appropriate context, of acceptance by the majority. Thus, a Bill of Rights could be enacted, entrenching minority freedoms, and the Republic could be given a carefully defined role in its enforcement. Offensive provisions such as the Flags and Emblems Act could be repealed, so that the law treated the Union Jack and the Irish tricolour on equal terms. The RUC could be made accountable to a strengthened police authority, which might consult representatives from the Republic. The trial of Republican terrorists by Diplock courts might be replaced by trial by jury on mainland Britain, or trial in Ireland by a pair of judges, one from the United Kingdom and one from the Republic.

Given the varied background and political views of the members, it was remarkable that the Committee was unanimous on a number of important topics. All were agreed that there should be greater involvement of the Government of the Republic in the enforcement of the law against terrorist crimes. All were agreed that such further involvement could not be required by the British Government unless it was willing to allow the Republic to be involved, in some degree, in other matters affecting the welfare of the minority community in Northern Ireland. There were disagreements, however, about the appropriate degree of Dublin involvement both in law enforcement itself and in the internal administration of the province. The final chapter of the Report, accordingly, presented two different models of possible co-operation between the Government of the Republic and the Government of the United Kingdom. The first model, commanding the support of a majority of the members, was called 'Co-operative Devolution'. The second model, which seemed more appropriate to a substantial minority of the members, was called 'Functional Co-operation'.

The members in the minority (which included David Howell, and Simon Jenkins, the political editor of *The Economist*) were apprehensive of the effect on Unionist opinion of any substantial Dublin involvement in Northern affairs. They recommended that responsibility for security within Northern Ireland should be discharged by the British Government alone, though a non-executive Joint Security Consultative Committee should be set up to advise the Secretary of State on such issues as the relative balance of police and army forces, and to channel greater co-operation between the Irish police or Garda and the RUC. There should also be a Standing Advisory Committee on Legal Matters to review developments in the civil liberties and human rights fields in the United Kingdom and the Republic, and review the areas where reciprocity between the Republic and the United Kingdom had been agreed or seemed desirable. There should be Joint Authorities in particular fields, but they must be the result of a genuine need for co-operation in limited areas such as industry, energy, tourism, transport and natural resources.

The Assembly, according to the Kilbrandon minority, should be given local government powers, but there should be no devolved executive. There could be a committee system, with places allocated proportionately but with each committee electing its own chairman. Power-sharing was rejected, but there could be entrenched clauses and weighted majorities, and the Secretary of State could intervene to break deadlocks.

The majority of the Committee favoured a greater degree of involvement of the Republic and a greater degree of devolved self-government. For this reason they called their option 'Co-operative Devolution'.

All members of the Committee had agreed that there should be closer co-operation between the two Governments in fighting terrorism, and all had agreed that there was need for a stronger police authority in Northern Ireland. The majority, however, wanted to offer a role to the Irish Government in the enforcement of law within Northern Ireland itself. They proposed that the new and strengthened police authority, to exercise control over the RUC, should include representation from the Republic. A possible form of such a co-operative police authority would consist of the Minister from the Northern Ireland Office responsible for security, the Minister of Justice or his deputy from the Republic of Ireland, and three representatives from Northern Ireland, two to represent the majority and one the minority communities. In due course these local representatives should be elected, but in current circumstances it would be appropriate for them to be nominated by the Secretary of State, in consultation with the authorities in the Republic of Ireland. They should be figures well known and respected in their communities. Units of the British Army, including the UDR, stationed in Northern Ireland to support the police, should be subject to this new co-operative police authority as the civil power in whose support they were acting. The Commission, in its turn, would be directly responsible to the Secretary of State, who would have power to overrule its decisions.

Co-operation in law enforcement must be, the Committee believed, combined with political co-operation. A combination of elements from the Forum proposals on joint authority, with existing provisions for the introduction of devolved government, constituted the model of co-operative devolution favoured by the majority of the Committee.

The Northern Ireland Act of 1973 had introduced the concept of 'rolling devolution', which provided that powers should be devolved to local institutions to the extent that they had proved themselves to enjoy the confidence of both local communities. No powers had ever been devolved to the Northern Ireland Assembly, in accordance with that Act, because it had never been recognised as acceptable by the minority.

On the other hand, the Unionists were surely correct in claiming that it was unacceptable that in Northern Ireland there are no indigenous representatives who decided and directed policy on major services and who themselves were answerable to their electorates for their steward-ship. Direct rule, whether from Westminster as at present, or from Dublin and London jointly, as proposed in the first of the Forum sub-committee models, was not a form of Government which is acceptable in the long-term. Some form of devolved Government was necessary. The difficulty was to devise a form of devolved Government which was not seen by the minority in the province as concentrating power in the hands of the majority, or vice versa.

The Sunningdale Agreement had tried to achieve this by the creation of a power-sharing executive: the Secretary of State was permitted to choose an executive from parties which appeared to him to command widespread support in the community. The prior provisions for 'rolling devolution' similarly provided for power to be devolved to the North-ern Ireland Assembly only if the Westminster Parliament was satisfied that an order for the devolution of particular powers was likely to command widespread acceptance throughout the community. On either system, the decision on the form of power-sharing was reserved to London; Fine Gael and the SDLP had favoured an approach which guaranteed a place as of right in any executive or cabinet to representa-tives of all major parties on the basis of proportional representation.

The weakness of these forms of power-sharing is that they do not provide mechanisms for the resolution of disputes within the Govern-ment. If the executive takes decision by majority votes, the majority ascendancy can be replicated within the Cabinet; if unanimity is required, the minority can hamstring the Government. Nor is it clear what happens if a section of the executive resigns or boycotts its meetings; no system of government can permit the refusal of a relatively small minority to co-operate to bring down the Government. It was notable that the Forum Report, in its provisions for a unitary state, did not propose power-sharing as a means of meeting the assumed desire of Northern Protestants to share in the Government of a new all-Ireland state.

Instead of power-sharing, the Kilbrandon majority proposed a system of co-operative devolution which was a modification of the concept of joint authority within the programme for rolling devolution. It combined two elements which were intended to have attractions for the two different sections of the community. It contained first a real measure of devolution of power to a democratically elected assembly and second the close involvement of the minority community in the administration of the North coupled with the initial co-operation of Dublin. Equally, it retained the 'direct rule' element of the presence of the Secretary of State for Northern Ireland, as recognition of a continued British security role and of the British Treasury's financial commitment to the province.

A devolved executive must be representative, it must have an effective decision procedure, and it must be made proof against boycott. The top tier of Government within the province proposed by the Kilbrandon majority was a five-man executive, consisting of the Secretary of State for Northern Ireland or his deputy, the Minister of Foreign Affairs of the Republic of Ireland or his deputy, and three members elected by the voters of Northern Ireland, in such a way that two of them were representative of the majority community, and one of them was representative of the minority.

One way in which the majority and minority members of such an executive could be chosen would be simply to appoint the members already elected to the European Parliament from the province. These had been elected by an unquestionably democratic procedure, and already had experience of working together to promote the interests of the province. It might, however, be thought that the doubling of duties would place too heavy a burden on them, or that the qualities needed to represent Northern Ireland in Europe might differ from those needed to operate a joint authority executive. If so, three members could be directly elected to the executive by a similar form of proportional representation. An executive constituted in either of these ways would be fairly representative: the majority would be represented two-to-one among the local members, and the minority plus their patron would be two-fifths of the body, which is approximately the proportion among the population.

Within the executive, a simple majority vote would provide an effective decision procedure (a majority of those present and voting). The constitution of the executive would be such that it could not be predicted that there would be a uniform voting pattern. No doubt there would be occasions on which a vote would be carried by the British and Unionist votes against the Nationalist and Irish vote. But nationalists had consistently preferred direct rule from Westminster to local Stormont majority rule: therefore, they recognised that there were occasions where Westminster would favour them against Unionists' wishes. In the executive, such a case would result in a measure being carried by the votes of the British, Irish and nationalist members against the opposition of the Unionists. In a manner of speaking, the British representative would have been holding the balance between Orange votes and Green votes: this would reflect the underlying reality of British sovereignty over a divided province, while allowing the fullest practical degree of sharing of power among local representatives. To cover all eventualities, the UK Government would no doubt wish to reserve a power of veto to its own representative.

In such an executive, if all the local members adopted a boycott, the default position was in effect joint rule directly by the London and Dublin members. This might be tolerable for a period until the new institutions won the confidence of local politicians. Indeed, it might well be thought that joint rule by London and Dublin was preferable to direct rule by London alone. But the Kilbrandon majority hoped that there would be little incentive for a single faction to boycott the executive while the others take their places. Boycotting the existing Assembly made tactical sense, because it stopped the rolling of devolution. A party which boycotted a Kilbrandon-type executive would forfeit its own share of power and leave local power in the hands of its opponents.

It could be hoped, then, that such a five-member executive would be representative, effective, and comparatively boycott-proof.

The powers to be given to such a devolved executive were not specified in detail by Kilbrandon: it was suggested that they should initially be modest, and be increased in the light of experience. At the full extent of devolution, the executive could decide on the allocation of resources to particular departments, within an overall budget to be determined by the UK Government. It could raise or rebate minor local taxes in addition to the principal taxes which would, as before, be fixed by Westminster. It could appoint ministers to run the departments which were placed under it, and be responsible for senior appointments within it.

At the fullness of its powers, the devolved executive should be concerned with the matters administered through the six Northern Ireland departments of Finance and Personnel, Economic Development, Environment, Agriculture, Education and Health and Social Services, and some or all of the powers reserved by the 1973 Act. If the executive were fully to gain the confidence of both communities, the Joint Security Commission might in due course be made subject to it.

The Kilbrandon majority considered that devolved government should have a legislative as well as an executive arm, since it was clearly, in their view, desirable that the administration of the province should be scrutinised by a locally-elected body. The Committee considered, and rejected, the suggestion that an inter-parliamentary tier should provide the legislature for Northern Ireland. Instead, it proposed that the existing Assembly should have the responsibility for scrutinising the conduct of the executive and the departmental ministers.

The Committee agreed with the Unionist proposals that the Assembly should be strengthened by giving it the local government powers proposed for the old Stormont by the Macrory Report. With an executive responsible for certain 'national' functions (e.g. Economic Development, Environment), the Assembly could be responsible broadly for the functions proposed by Macrory, and since it should continue in existence at least for local government functions, it would be the natural local body to which the proposed executive should be subject to scrutiny. This should be, so the Kilbrandon majority considered, not on the basis of rolling devolution, but on the basis of a clear statement by the British Government of a determination to return specific powers to the new executive and specific powers to the Assembly. Nothing less than this would reassure the majority community of the Government's commitment to the revival of democracy in the province and to a measure of restored self-rule.

Co-operative devolution could only be made acceptable if it was clearly accepted as a durable solution, and not as a method of coercing Unionists into a united Ireland. The solution must be transparent: there must be no 'hidden agenda', in the words of Peter Barry, 'to be the focus of fear or suspicions'. This did not mean that any package agreed between the parties must come into force immediately, once and for all; but it meant that its possible evolution should be clearly set out in advance.

The recommendations concluded with the following remarks.

12.29. This means that every possible care must be taken to enshrine the agreement in a form which is formal, transparent, and definitive. We believe, as does the Forum subcommittee, that the most appropriate form would be a Treaty between the two Governments, terminable, with due notice, by either side, but deposited with the United Nations. Throughout the duration of the Treaty, sovereignty will remain with the United Kingdom, and should it be revoked, all powers conferred on representatives of the Irish Government will revert to the U.K. Government.

12.30. How long should the Treaty last? The Forum subcommittee report (para 54) says, 'It could be argued that if joint authority is justified where there is a nationalist minority of 35–40%, it would be equally justified where there was a substantial Unionist minority in the North.' Most of us believe that this argument is correct, and that any modified form of joint authority that was adopted should continue if there should be a majority in Northern Ireland who favoured a United Ireland, even though sovereignty might pass from London to Dublin when a majority voted for such a change. We believe that this should be affirmed, in an appropriate way, in the Treaty.

12.31. The most dramatic step which the Irish Government could

take to exhibit good faith to Unionists, to make the treaty transparent, and to remove suspicions of any coercion into a unitary
state, would be to repeal or amend Articles 2 and 3 of the Irish
Constitution.

12.32. Some of us hope that the operation of co-operative devolution would lead Unionists to accept movement towards some
model of Irish unity. If successful, co-operative devolution may so
change the climate of opinion in the North that further political
changes may then be introduced. Others of us are sceptical about
this. But all of us are in agreement that any such movement must
be by genuine conversion to the idea on the part of Unionists: not
by any form of coercion or mere demographic change. If any of the
reforms we have considered are to work they must be seen as something which could work indefinitely and on its merits and not
simply as a stepping stone to a United Ireland. However, some of
us believe that a successful form of joint authority may so change
the climate of opinion in the North that further political changes
may then be introduced.

12.33. Is there any hope that co-operative devolution would be
acceptable to Unionists? We believe that from the proposals we
have considered a package could be put together which would offer
positive advantages to Unionists. In the first place, it would offer
their elected representatives a real part in the government of their
country. We agree with the Unionist 'The Way Forward' that this
has been too long denied them. In the second place, the guarantee
that they would remain part of the United Kingdom until a
majority of the people of Northern Ireland voted otherwise would
not merely be retained; it would be strengthened by becoming a
bilateral guarantee enshrined in a treaty between the United
Kingdom and the Irish Republic. Thirdly, the minority safeguards
involved in co-operative devolution could be automatically transferred to the Unionists if they should become the minority in
Northern Ireland. Finally, by offering nationalists a substantial
recognition of their Irish identity it would enable Unionists to fulfil
what 'The Way Foward' calls 'The responsibility of the majority to
persuade the minority that the Province is also theirs'. By doing so

it would contribute to the long-term peace and stability for which constitutional nationalists and Unionists are both striving.

14.

'Out, Out, Out'

The Kilbrandon Report, which appeared on the day Mrs Gandhi was assassinated, did not attract much public attention. It was denounced in the Republican Irish Press for pointing back in the direction of Stormont, a Stormont with tighter control from Britain, and a token Southerner on the executive for the look of things. In Unionist circles a single sentence from the Report was seized on: paragraph 10.11 had recommended a substantial increase in the establishment of the RUC and added, 'This would permit a gradual running down of the part-time Ulster Defence Regiment as the RUC took over more security functions.' This proposal, according to the *Belfast Newsletter*, defied logic; and the suggestion that full-time members of the UDR might be incorporated in the British Army verged on 'an insult to those who day and daily put their lives on the line to protect the innocent in this troubled community'.

In the Northern Ireland Assembly on 15 November Mr Frank Millar proposed a motion

> That this Assembly rejects the recommendations of the independent inquiry chaired by Lord Kilbrandon, and in particular the recommendations set forth in paragraph 11 of chapter 10 concerning the future role of the Royal Ulster Constabulary.

The motion was partly an excuse to discuss without violating the terms of reference of the Assembly the role of the security forces. But Mr Millar, while imputing good intentions to the members of the Inquiry, considered that unwittingly they had become parties to dark Republican designs. He lamented that with regard to the UDR not only members of the Inquiry but 'some very senior officers in the Royal

Ulster Constabulary would appear to have bought this particular line of Republican propaganda'.

Mr Jim Allister of the DUP was far more critical. 'Having studied this report, parts of which are so fantastic and so outrageous, I am tempted to wonder whether it even merits serious debate. It would be easy of course to dismiss it as the rantings of lofty academics, but perhaps in reality it is more the poison of malevolent academics.' The Inquiry was abused for having countenanced the suggestion that there had been discrimination against Catholics in Northern Ireland; for being insufficiently explicit in denouncing articles 2 and 3 of the Irish Constitution; and for suggesting that the Government might have adopted a more flexible attitude with regard to Republican hunger strikers. Particularly obnoxious was the proposal to repeal the Flags and Emblems Act. To legalise the flying of the Irish tricolour was out of the question. 'Every time it is hoisted is an affirmation of articles 2 and 3 of the Irish Constitution.' Mr Allister concluded by threatening that if any attempt was made to implement co-operative devolution on the Kilbrandon model there would be unrest which would put 1974 in the shade. The proposals were dismissed as 'fantasy and green dreams' and 'lunacy'.

Mr Cushnahan, of the Alliance party, observed that 'There are not many things which unite Northern Ireland politicians, but Kilbrandon seems to be one of the exceptions.' He paid compliments to the members of the committee, and welcomed their rejection of the three Forum models, but concluded that 'the major recommendations of the Kilbrandon Report quite clearly are unrealistic, are divorced from the realities of the Northern Ireland problem, and therefore do not, in their own way, offer a sensible framework for discussion'.

Mr Robinson, Deputy Leader of the DUP, agreed with the negative judgement of the Kilbrandon Report. He did, however, offer the authors of the report an excuse: the real blame lay elsewhere, in the terms of reference. 'If you have to comment on a document that is absolute nonsense — as the New Ireland Forum Report was — then naturally your document will be nonsense.'

Four days after this Assembly debate Dr FitzGerald and Mrs Thatcher met at Chequers in the second summit of the Anglo-Irish Intergovernmental Council. They published a communiqué, reaffirm-

ing the position of the two Governments with regard to Northern
Ireland in the terms traditional since Sunningdale, and then added:

> The Taoiseach and the Prime Minister agreed that:
> (i)   Any attempt to promote political objectives by means of vio-
>   lence or the threat of violence must be rejected, as must those
>   who adopt or support such methods.
> (ii) The identities of both the majority and minority communi-
>   ties in Northern Ireland should be recognised and respected,
>   and reflected in the structures and processes of Northern
>   Ireland in ways acceptable to both communities.
> (iii) The process of government in Northern Ireland should be
>   such as to provide the people of both communities with the
>   confidence that their rights will be safeguarded.
> (iv) Co-operation between their two Governments in matters of
>   security should be maintained and where possible improved.

The public's attention did not delay long upon these admirable sentiments: it was soon diverted elsewhere. During a press conference after
the Summit, Mrs Thatcher was asked for her opinion of the three main
options in the Forum Report. She replied:

> I have made it quite clear — and so did Mr Prior when he was
> Secretary of State for Northern Ireland — that a unified Ireland
> was one solution that is out. A second solution was confederation
> of two states. That is out. A third solution was joint authority.
> That is out. That is a derogation from sovereignty. We made that
> quite clear when the Report was published.

The Prime Minister's press conference caused consternation in the
Republic of Ireland. It was not so much the content of the statement
which caused distress: after all, the Irish Prime Minister himself had
repeatedly said that the three models sketched in the Forum Report
were not the only possible ways forward. And Mrs Thatcher was merely
echoing Mr Prior's rejection of the Forum proposals, which was a rejection qualified with the phrase 'inasmuch as any of the models significantly alters the sovereignty of Northern Ireland'. What gave offence
was the trenchant and forthright manner of the rejection. The normally
restrained *Irish Times* said of Mrs Thatcher, 'She is as offhand and

patronising as she is callous and imperious.' Irishmen felt that the Taoiseach had been humiliated, and grieved or rejoiced according to their politics. Dr FitzGerald himself had good reason to be pleased with the progress made in private at the summit, and was able to report to the Dail that the discussions had reached 'a crucial and critical stage'. Unionist fears were lulled by the Prime Minister's counting out of the Forum options. Peter Robinson of the DUP described it as 'a neutral summit', constrained by the Brighton bombing. 'There was nothing either for or against minority or majority interests', he said. 'They don't want to be seen to be giving in to the IRA by giving in to the minority, nor are they punishing them because of the IRA bombing. We have to hold our breath until the next summit.'

Before the next summit a debate in the House of Lords on 3 December 1984 gave the Government an opportunity to soften the harsh impression made in Ireland by the Prime Minister's press conference. Lord Underhill invited the Government to give their views on the Kilbrandon Report, which he commended to the House. Several peers associated themselves with the main lines of the report, and Lord Lyell, for the Government, took a stance between the Kilbrandon majority and minority.

The longest intervention was by Lord Fitt who was sceptical:

> I believe that it will be damned difficult, but that it will be possible in some way to resurrect the power-sharing arrangements we had in 1974. But I am totally and absolutely convinced — though the fact that I am convinced in my own mind does not make me a Unionist — that any involvement by way of the Government of the Republic would totally kill any hope of the communities getting together in the North.

'I commend those who took part in drawing up this report,' he concluded. 'It is a reasonable document — that is why it is not accepted in Ireland: because the more unreasonable you are over there the more success you are guaranteed electorally.'

15.

Positive Proposals

When the summit of November 1984 broke up, it was intended that the two Prime Ministers should meet again within a few months. But reaching conclusions on the form the agreement should take was a matter of much more work than was anticipated. It was not for a whole year, until November 1985, that the ground had been fully prepared. In the meantime, a number of bodies, official and unofficial, offered advice to the two Governments on how they should proceed.

One of the most helpful contributions to the debate was the Penguin Special *Ireland: A Positive Proposal* by Kevin Boyle and Tom Hadden, completed in May 1985 and published a few months later. The authors had worked together for many years on the operation of the emergency laws in Northern Ireland; they made a joint submission to the New Ireland Forum. Both of them were, by birth, Northern Irishmen: Hadden, from Loyalist Portadown, now a lecturer in law at Queen's University; Boyle, from Nationalist Newry, now Professor of Law at University College, Galway.

Two key principles guided the proposals in their book. First, one of the roots of the present problem was the failure of the Republic and Britain to agree and commit themselves fully to a single view on the constitutional status of Northern Ireland. Secondly, proposals for allowing any exercise of power by the Republic of Ireland in the North could only be acceptable on the basis that any joint powers should operate in a reciprocal manner on both sides of the border.

Thus the first requirement for resolving the Northern Ireland problem was a decision by the British and Irish states to realign their relationship over a territory that was once in dispute between them so as to emphasise current realities rather than historic enmities. A new treaty could be drawn up containing the following provisions:

The Governments of the United Kingdom and of the Republic of Ireland, recognising that Northern Ireland is a territory in which there are two communities with divided loyalties and in which special arrangements are required to ensure that those loyalties can be fully expressed . . . have therefore resolved:

(1) to take further measures to secure the common concerns of their peoples and to ensure co-operation and harmony in future relations without prejudice to the independence or the sovereign rights of both states;

(2) that there shall be no change in the constitutional status of Northern Ireland as part of the United Kingdom until a majority of the people in Northern Ireland desire a change;

(3) that appropriate measures shall be taken by both sides to guarantee the rights and interests of both communities in Northern Ireland and that if at any time in the future a majority of the people of Northern Ireland should vote to join a united Ireland, corresponding measures shall be taken by both states to guarantee the rights and interests of both communities within a unitary Irish state.

The treaty should also contain resolutions to develop social, economic and cultural policy, and to deal more effectively with terrorism. Boyle and Hadden suggested ways in which this could be done in accordance with the principle of reciprocity.

The procedures for extra-territorial jurisdiction agreed after Sunningdale gave an example of how reciprocal arrangements can work. According to that agreement, persons charged with any serious offence can be tried either in Northern Ireland or in the Republic, wherever the offence was committed; evidence can be heard in the other jurisdiction by the judge concerned if any witness refuses to appear in the trial court. Thus Irish judges can hear evidence in Belfast, and Northern Ireland judges can hear evidence in Dublin.

Boyle and Hadden suggested that this principle of reciprocity should be extended. A limited cross-border security zone could be set up in which members of the police forces of both sides, by agreement, could operate for purposes of preventive action or surveillance. It would be possible for a judge, or legal assessor, from the other jurisdiction to sit in court in any case with a cross-border element, whether arising from extradition, extraterritorial jurisdiction, or cross-border patrolling. There might eventually be a single cross-border court to deal with prescribed terrorist offences on either side of the border. Any of these proposals would obviously need to operate under some intergovernmental security committee.

According to Boyle and Hadden, an Anglo-Irish interparliamentary tier should be given the role of monitoring progress within Northern Ireland on the various aspects of an overall settlement. Within Northern Ireland itself three main ways of providing for full and equal recognition of the two communities were proposed. First, Northern Irish citizens who wish to do so must be given formal recognition of their right to be Irish, by accepting and exercising Irish citizenship. They should be allowed joint membership of British and Irish parliamentary institutions, and the Flags and Emblems Act should be repealed. Secondly, much better provision must be made for the protection of individual and communal rights within Northern Ireland, perhaps by a general Bill of Rights. Thirdly, arrangements must be made for the participation of the minority in Government. On this Boyle and Hadden write:

> Since the arrangements for internal government within Northern Ireland are clearly crucial to any lasting settlement, some more realistic system than the highly discretionary provisions for 'power-sharing' is clearly required. The most practical approach would be to provide that both legislation and other governmental decisions needing a formal administrative order should require a weighted majority of votes in any regional assembly or parliament in respect of matters of particular communal concern, such as education, local government, policing and security, the location of major industrial developments and all matters of an electoral or constitutional nature. It would not be necessary to require the same weighted majority for all these matters. A 60 per cent vote might be thought sufficient for some decisions, while other more fundamental and constitutional matters might require a 75 per cent vote. The principle that different types of decision require different majorities is well-established in the constitutions of other countries.

Boyle and Hadden finally faced the question whether it would ever be possible to get support for a carefully balanced settlement recognising the legitimate claims of both communities. They concluded that it would, if the British and Irish Governments made clear that they would press ahead with the parts of the programme that do not need local political support. They should try to get a sufficiently broad spectrum of local parties to co-operate and failing that to rely on a referendum, asking voters to choose between a proposed cross-communal settlement and continuing direct rule on a first- and second-choice basis.

In July 1985 there appeared a report prepared for the leaders of the two British Alliance parties, the Liberals and the SDP. The committee which prepared the report was chaired by Lord Donaldson, and included Shirley Williams and David Alton MP. The report was entitled *What Future for Northern Ireland?*

Like the Forum and the Kilbrandon Committee, the Alliance Commission accepted that no internal settlement in Northern Ireland could succeed unless a role were found for the Irish Republic in the settlement of the Northern Ireland problem. Three principles were enunciated at the outset: both Unionist and Nationalist traditions were legitimate and valid; Northern Ireland should not cease to be part of the United Kingdom without the consent of the majority; and there must be institutions which allowed members of both communities to play a part in the government of Northern Ireland. No divided society could be successfully governed without some form of partnership in government. But in addition to partnership in government, institutional recognition of the 'Irish Dimension' was necessary. This should be done by a link between the United Kingdom and the Irish Republic, rather than between Northern Ireland and the Irish Republic, as foreshadowed in the abortive experiment of 1974. Hence the most appropriate form for the East–West link to take would be a British–Irish Parliamentary Council, perhaps leading eventually to a confederal arrangement embracing the entire British Isles. For the immediate battle against terrorism, there should be a joint British–Irish Security Commission.

Since the failure of power-sharing in 1974, any proposal for partnership in government has to be carefully thought out and convincingly argued. The Alliance proposal differed from the 1974 model in three ways: the Executive was to be chosen by the Assembly, not chosen by the Secretary of State; no cabinet system of collective responsibility was involved; and the system was to be designed to survive a series of elections leading to variations in party strengths. The proposed structure comprised the following elements: an Assembly of 102 members (six from each of the present Westminster constituencies, elected by proportional representation); an executive committee of ten members elected, by proportional representation, by the Assembly; a Chief Minister to head the Executive, with each of the remaining members a departmental minister; and a series of Assembly committees, one for each department chaired by the appropriate minister. Assembly members standing for election to the Executive would have to make a declaration renouncing violence.

Under this system the Assembly would be the legislature for all matters except the reserved and excepted matters (including security, the judicial system, and the electoral franchise) which would continue to be controlled by Westminster. The legislative initiative within the Assembly would come from the ministers and their committees, though proposals would need budgetary approval from the Executive Committee before being drafted into a Bill. The Commission's report explored various ways in which the provisions might break down, and sought to safeguard against this. But it argued, on the basis of opinion polls conducted in 1980, 1981 and 1984, that a Northern Ireland Assembly, with guarantees for Catholics, within the United Kingdom was a constitutional option acceptable to a majority of both Catholics and Protestants. A referendum could be held, if necessary, before the system was introduced. But in the last resort, if efforts were made to sabotage the new system, an Alliance Government must be willing and ready to deploy the full force of the state to prevent the disruption of constitutional government.

The British-Irish Parliamentary Council proposed by the Alliance was to be consultative and deliberative: its purpose would be to improve relations between the entire United Kingdom and the Irish Republic, recognising the interdependence of the economies of the two countries and the advantages to be gained by the two Governments jointly advancing schemes for economic and social development to be submitted to the European Commission and European Parliament. The

British–Irish Parliamentary Council should be modelled on the Nordic Council which has achieved cultural, economic, legal and social co-operation between the five sovereign states of Denmark, Finland, Iceland, Norway and Sweden. The Nordic Council has been more successful than the European Community in harmonising legislation, and it has achieved its successes despite the fact that two of its members are neutral states and three belong to NATO. Within the Nordic Council, special representation is given to the Aland Islands and to the Faroes, even though these are parts of Finland and Denmark respectively: similarly, within a British–Irish Council there should be an over-representation of Northern Ireland. In a Council of twenty-nine members, twelve could be drawn from the Irish Republic, twelve from Great Britain, and five from Northern Ireland. The members would be appointed by the sovereign Parliaments, from their own number or from the Northern Ireland Assembly. The Council would examine legislation submitted by the two Governments on matters of common concern, with the powers of select committees to send for persons and papers. It would also be able to conduct investigations of its own on matters affecting relations between the two countries, or between communities within them; and it would have a role in long-term planning for cross-border economic development.

The third of the Alliance Commission's main proposals was the setting up of a joint British–Irish Security Commission. Closer co-operation between Dublin and Westminster in the fight against terrorism was necessary not only as an operational requirement but also in order to secure trust and support for the security forces in the North from the Catholic minority there. Echoing the Forum and Kilbrandon, the Commission said: 'Support in defeating the IRA from members of the minority in the North will not be forthcoming so long as the RUC is seen as the representative of an authority with which the minority cannot openly identify.' But it is equally important that the majority's support should not be weakened, and therefore 'reforms in the organisation of the security forces should be capable of being justified as a necessary step towards making them more effective in the war against terrorism, and not as a covert attempt to alter the constitutional status of Northern Ireland'.

The particular reforms proposed by the Alliance included the streng-

thening of the Police Authority, which is responsible for the super-
vision of the RUC. This should be given greater powers, including the
power to draw up general provisions governing the routing of marches
and demonstrations; and an elected element should be introduced in
place of the present totally nominated body. In order to move in the
direction of community policing — impossible in a divided and intimi-
dated community — statutory police liaison committees should be
established. Members of these committees, as of the Assembly
Executive, would be required to make a declaration committing themselves to democratic methods and the renunciation of violence. The
Alliance Commission judged the present complaints procedure
deficient in several respects, the most important being that complaints
are investigated by officers of the RUC, the very force against which the
complaint is alleged. An essential reform was that a wholly independent
body should be established with the task of investigating all complaints
against the police. In particular, there must be appropriate machinery
for dealing with cases where it is alleged that the security forces have
caused death or serious injury. An independent standing tribunal
should be set up and required to investigate every such case; it should
have a legally qualified chairman and a membership appointed by the
Secretary of State; it should have power to compel witnesses to appear
and give evidence on oath. The instructions issued to the security forces
concerning the use of force ('The Yellow Card') should be published;
and the general principle, that lethal force should only be used when
necessary to save life or prevent serious injury, should be given precise
form in detailed rules. Despite considerable cross-community support
in opinion polls for combined British–Irish security patrols on both
sides of the border, the Alliance considered such co-operation between
the two police forces impracticable at present, but it called for joint
studies and reciprocal police training through the exchange of officers
between Northern Ireland and the Republic.

Like all other bodies who have seriously studied the implications of
the slogan 'Troops Out', the Alliance Commission came to the conclusion that the withdrawal of British troops, whether immediately or at
some specified future date, would be unlikely to contribute to the just
and stable government of Northern Ireland. But it welcomed the progress made recently in reducing the number of troops in the province,

and the number of occasions on which they are committed in support of the police. It hoped that the complete withdrawal of the Army from West Belfast, if not from the border, might shortly be possible. On the topic of the UDR, the Commission, perturbed by the number of convictions of UDR personnel for murder, manslaughter and assault, had this to say:

> We accept that the UDR not infrequently creates hostility amongst the Catholic community comparable to that formerly felt towards the 'B' specials. In the context of the policy of normalising the security situation in Northern Ireland, and lessening the Army presence, we believe that the UDR should be phased out as soon as possible. We understand, however, that the Regiment is at present carrying out duties which it would take eight Battalions of regular British troops to cover. Thus the phasing out can only be gradual, as part of the general policy which has reduced that Army presence from 22,000 in 1972 to 9500 now. But some priority should be given to reducing the UDR numbers at once, starting perhaps with the part-timers. Meanwhile, more should be done to improve the training of full-time members of the Regiment. Secondment to units of the Regular Army and courses at Army training establishments might be valuable means to that end. . . .
>
> The duties currently undertaken by the UDR should progressively be taken over by the RUC whose establishment would need to be increased accordingly. With regard to the UDR, we place on record that we do not wish to see this form of policing continued in the United Kingdom or any part of it. For, in the words of the Hunt Report, 'Policing in a free society depends on a wide measure of public approval and consent. This has never been obtained in the long-term by military or para-military means.'

In addition to the three major proposals for the Government-partnership Executive, the British–Irish Parliamentary Council, and the Joint Security Commission, the Alliance proposed a number of detailed reforms, particularly in the area of emergency powers and civil liberties. The Commission accepted reluctantly that in present conditions jury trials for terrorist offences were not possible in Northern Ireland, but it recommended that non-jury trials should be conducted not by a

single judge, as at present, but by three judges, as in the Special
Criminal Courts in the Irish Republic. Moreover, the number of
defendants in any one trial should never exceed six. The Commission
was also concerned at delays in bringing suspects to trial: in 1983 the
average prisoner refused bail had to wait 322 days before being tried. It
recommended that where delay was caused by the prosecution, the
defendant should automatically be entitled to bail or release after 110
days in custody.

The Commission hoped that the introduction of three-judge panels,
the reduction in the size of trials, and statutory limits on remands in
custody, would remove much of the anxiety expressed about Diplock
courts. But too many offences were currently 'scheduled', i.e. defined
by the Emergency Provisions Act as being matter for non-jury courts; it
had been claimed in a recent independent study that no less than 40 per
cent of those tried by the Diplock courts had no apparent connection
with terrorism. Minor offences should be descheduled, and the accused
in any particular case should have the right to apply to the court to have
his case descheduled. Where special powers of arrest or search are exercised under emergency legislation, it should not suffice that the security
forces merely suspected a citizen of being a terrorist: the standard
should be one of reasonable suspicion. Confessions obtained from suspects should be admissible as evidence only if it could be clearly shown
that they had not been the results of physical violence or the threat of it
by the police. Altogether the emergency legislation must be clearly seen
to be just that: interim, undesirable provision to be maintained only as
long as terrorism continues. The Prevention of Terrorism Act should
be replaced as soon as possible by legislation jointly agreed by the
British and Irish Governments and applicable in both countries.

In the area of civil liberties and human rights, the Alliance Commission joined the long list of bodies which have recommended that a Bill
of Rights should be enacted for Northern Ireland. The simplest way of
doing this, the Commission argued, would be to incorporate into
domestic law the European Convention on Human Rights: preferably
for the whole United Kingdom, but if this is impossible, then for
Northern Ireland alone. This would obviate endless argument about
what a special Bill would contain; but, the Commission noted, in the
particular conditions of Northern Ireland it might be necessary to add a

wider non-discrimination clause than the European Convention now provides. The enforcement of the rights thus to be conceded should not be left to individual initiative alone: a new Commission on Human Rights in Northern Ireland should be set up to oversee the legislation, assist litigants, and propose changes where necessary. This could take over the functions of three already existing agencies already concerned with human rights: the Fair Employment Agency, the Equal Opportunities Commission and the Standing Advisory Commission on Human Rights. An aspect of human rights which should not be overlooked is respect for the culture and traditions of different groups: in this context the Commission called for the repeal of the Flags and Emblems Act and the provision prohibiting street signs in Gaelic.

After making some proposals for increased economic co-operation between the British and Irish Governments within the context of the European Community, the Alliance Commission Report concluded with a brief consideration of the longer-term prospect of relations between the islands of the British–Irish archipelago. It was important that British governments should consider long-term objectives, because there was a danger that a British electorate, weary of the human and financial costs of continuing the Union, might withdraw from Northern Ireland without waiting for any consent by the majority there. This, the Commission said, would only reproduce on an all-Ireland scale the troubles which have existed for so long in Northern Ireland. Relations between the United Kingdom and the Republic were already uniquely close: religious, trade union, banking and sporting bonds are closer across the border than they are across the Irish Sea; all citizens of the Republic have the same rights as citizens of the United Kingdom; almost all people in Northern Ireland are citizens also of the Irish state. It is with this in mind that future relationships should be considered; and the Alliance Commission concluded:

> It is difficult to predict how the relationship between the United Kingdom and the Irish Republic would evolve after partnership government becomes a reality, but one of the institutional forms which this relationship could take might be a confederal one. This would provide institutional recognition of the fact that, as well as the political links, there are also deep personal and cultural inter-relationships between our two countries.

After the full and detailed proposals that had been made by the Kilbrandon Committee, Boyle and Hadden, and the Alliance parties, the third and final report of the Northern Ireland Assembly Devolution Report Committee was a disappointment in its brevity and the paucity of its content. The proposals it contains are known as the Catherwood proposals, because Sir Frederick Catherwood was invited by the Assembly to write a report to provide a working basis for negotiations. The report produced in October 1985 contains less than three pages.

The report recommends that the legislative and executive responsibilities previously transferred under the 1973 Act should be exercised by the Assembly and devolved administration answerable to it. Negotiations should start with the Secretary of State on the role of the Assembly on law and order. The initial administration in a new Assembly should require a vote of confidence of two-thirds of the members; for the second administration, 55 per cent should suffice. If the threshold could not be reached, the Secretary of State could sanction an administration with simple majority support 'if he were satisfied that such an administration was likely to command widespread acceptance throughout the community'. Thereafter, a simple majority would operate.

The executive should continue to be matched by a committee system, with the allocation of members of committees proportional to their membership of the Assembly. The allocation of chairmen should reflect the strength of the parties by the order in which they are given, successively, the choice of chairs they want. A Bill of Rights should be entrenched in the new Constitution, and a procedure for appeal established. Thirty per cent of the Assembly should be able to require the Secretary of State to refer any proposed legislation to the Judicial Committee to test its validity from the point of view of discriminatoriness. The separate systems of education and the desire for expression of different cultures could be written into the Constitution.

16.

The Hillsborough Agreement

On 15 November 1985 Mrs Thatcher and Dr FitzGerald met at Hillsborough Castle outside Belfast. It was the third of the series of meetings of heads of government in the Anglo-Irish Intergovernmental Council. Hillsborough was the venue of an agreement which significantly altered the relationship between the two countries by providing for a new Intergovernmental Conference concerned with Northern Ireland and with relations between the two parts of the island of Ireland. The two premiers signed a formal and binding agreement whose aims were declared, in a joint communiqué, to be 'promoting peace and stability in Northern Ireland; helping to reconcile the two major traditions in Ireland; creating a new climate of friendship and co-operation between the people of the two countries; and improving co-operation in combatting terrorism'.

The objectives of the agreement, as set out in its preamble, were such as must command almost universal support; but it is notable that even in the preamble a certain bias can be detected in the tone and language. The choice of words and concepts depends heavily on the Forum's analysis of the problems of the province. The two traditions to be reconciled, for instance, are described not as 'Catholic' and 'Protestant', but as Unionist and Nationalist. The traditions are said to be 'represented on the one hand by those who wish for no change in the present status of Northern Ireland and on the other hand by those who aspire to a sovereign united Ireland achieved by peaceful means and through agreement'. Thus the Hillsborough agreement, like the Forum, defines its terms in such a way as to elide the significant number of Catholics who prefer to remain in the United Kingdom rather than to become part of the united Ireland.

The first article of the Anglo-Irish agreement concerns the constitutional status of Northern Ireland. It reads as follows:

The two governments
(a) affirm that any change in the status of Northern Ireland would only come about with the consent of a majority of the people of Northern Ireland;
(b) recognise that the present wish of a majority of the people of Northern Ireland is for no change in the status of Northern Ireland;
(c) declare that, if in the future a majority of the people of Northern Ireland clearly wish for and formally consent to the establishment of a united Ireland, they will introduce and support in the respective Parliaments legislation to give effect to that wish.

The wording of this first article has received, and repays, careful scrutiny. Notice first, that it speaks of *change* in the status of Northern Ireland: it does not determine the present status. It would indeed be difficult for the two governments, without risking challenge in their respective courts, to say what the present status is. For Irish law that status is spelt out in articles 2 and 3 of the Constitution; for United Kingdom law it is set out in the Northern Ireland Constitution Act 1973 which says 'Northern Ireland remains part of Her Majesty's Dominions and of the United Kingdom, and it is hereby affirmed that in no event will Northern Ireland or any part of it cease to be part of Her Majesty's dominions and of the United Kingdom without the consent of the majority of the people of Northern Ireland.' At Sunningdale the status of Northern Ireland was dealt with not by a joint statement of the two governments, but by a pair of parallel declarations. The Irish declaration was tantamount to article 1 (a) of the Hillsborough accord: the English declaration included a statement tantamount to 1 (c) of Hillsborough. But the English declaration at Sunningdale included the sentence 'The present status of Northern Ireland is that it is part of the United Kingdom.' Unionist readers of the Anglo-Irish agreement could regard article 1 (b) as a weakening of the Sunningdale statement; nationalists, on the other hand, could point out that 1 (b) represented an advance on the part of the Irish Government, which had made no such recognition at Sunningdale. Unionist suspicions were further fuelled when it was noted that copies of the agreement available in Dublin and London had different titles. The eastern party to the agreement was described in London as the 'government of the United Kingdom of Great Britain and Northern Ireland'; in Dublin it was merely described as the 'government of the United Kingdom'. There was further Unionist excitement when it was discovered that Dick Spring, the Tanaiste or Deputy Prime Minister in the Irish Coalition Government, had described Mrs Thatcher, when notifying members of his party about the agreement, as 'the Prime Minister of Great Britain'.

In fact the ambiguities of article 1 of the Hillsborough agreement do not represent any sinister weakening of the constitutional position of Northern Ireland in the United Kingdom, nor any bad faith on the part of the negotiators, British or Irish. They merely reflect the anxiety to avoid any constitutional challenge to the agreement, and witness to the baneful effect which articles 2 and 3 of the Irish Constitution have upon even the most friendly negotiations. It would have been much better if both states could have adopted in their internal legislation identical wording on the status of Northern Ireland.

A more substantial weakness in article 1 is that it makes no provision for the problems which would remain if, by a small majority, the population of the province were to vote to enter a united Ireland. As Harold McCusker was to point out in the House of Commons, if — as the whole philosophy of the agreement supposes — simple majority rule is not appropriate in Northern Ireland, why should any Unionist accept that a simple majority should take a Unionist out of his citizenship of the United Kingdom and into a united Ireland?

The draft treaty between the two governments proposed by Boyle and Hadden a few months before Hillsborough would have been more explicit on both these points. It read, in the relevant part, that it was agreed

> That there shall be no change in the constitutional status of Northern Ireland as part of the United Kingdom until a majority of the people of Northern Ireland desire a change; that appropriate measures shall be taken by both states to guarantee the rights and

interests of both communities in Northern Ireland and that if at any time in the future a majority of the people in Northern Ireland should vote to join a united Ireland, corresponding measures shall be taken by both states to guarantee the rights and interests of both communities within a unitary Irish state.

Such wording would not only have been clearer: it would also have been perfectly compatible with the principles of the New Ireland Forum, at least as interpreted by Fine Gael and Labour.

It was not, however, article 1 but article 2 of the Treaty which was seen, by friends and foes alike, as the cornerstone of the agreement. This established, within the framework of the Anglo-Irish Intergovernmental Council, an Intergovernmental Conference concerned with Northern Ireland and with relations between the two parts of Ireland, to deal on a regular basis with political matters, security and related matters, legal matters, including the administration of justice, and the promotion of cross-border co-operation. The basis of the conference was set out thus:

> The United Kingdom Government accept that the Irish Government will put forward views and proposals on matters relating to Northern Ireland within the field of activity of the Conference in so far as those matters are not the responsibility of a devolved administration in Northern Ireland. In the interests of promoting peace and stability, determined efforts shall be made through the Conference to resolve any differences. . . . There is no derogation from the sovereignty of either the United Kingdom Government or the Irish Government, and each retains responsibility for the decisions and administration of government within its own jurisdiction.

There were to be regular and frequent meetings of the conference at ministerial level as well as at official level. The ministerial meetings were to be chaired by the Secretary of State for Northern Ireland jointly with 'a Minister designated as the Permanent Irish Ministerial Representative' who has been, in the event, the Minister for Foreign Affairs, Mr Peter Barry TD. There was to be a secretariat to service the Conference on a continuing basis. No location was specified in the agreement, but the Secretariat had been established at Maryfield in Belfast.

In article 4 of the agreement, both governments declared their support for a policy of devolution.

It is the declared policy of the United Kingdom Government that responsibility in respect of certain matters within the power of the Secretary of State for Northern Ireland should be devolved within Northern Ireland on a basis which would secure widespread acceptance throughout the community. The Irish Government support that policy.

The Conference was to be a framework in which the Irish Government could put forward views and proposals on the modalities of devolution, in so far as they related to the interests of the minority community. As stated in article 2, if a devolved administration should be established, the devolved matters would not be for consideration by the Conference.

Article 5 spelt out the area of concern of the conference in political matters, concerning the rights and identities of the two traditions, 'to protect human rights and to prevent discrimination'. The area was widely defined: it would include measures to foster cultural heritage, changes in electoral arrangements, the use of flags and emblems, and the avoidance of economic and social discrimination. It would consider the advantages and disadvantages of a Bill of Rights for Northern Ireland. In the absence of devolution, the Irish Government may, where the interests of the minority community were significantly or especially affected, 'put forward views and proposals for major legislation and on major policy issues, which are within the purview of the Northern Ireland Departments, and which remain the responsibility of the Secretary of State for Northern Ireland'. A significant addition specified that 'the possible application of any measures pursuant to this Article by the Irish Government in their jurisdiction shall not be excluded'. It is unfortunate that this point was not developed with greater prominence in the interests of reciprocity and even-handedness.

Article 6 allowed for the Irish Government to put forward 'views and proposals on the role and composition' of such bodies as the Standing Advisory Commission on Human Rights, the Fair Employment Agency, the Equal Opportunities Commission, the Police Authority and the Police Complaints Board in Northern Ireland. Article 7 provided for the conference to consider security policy, relations between the security forces and the community, and prisons policy. It stated that 'there is a need for a programme of special measures in Northern Ireland to improve relations between the security forces and the community, with the object in particular of making the security forces more readily accepted by the nationalist community'.

The eighth article, concerning legal matters, read as follows:

> The Conference shall deal with issues of concern to both countries relating to the enforcement of the criminal law. In particular it shall consider whether there are areas of the criminal law applying in the North and in the South respectively which might with benefit be harmonised. The two Governments agree on the importance of public confidence in the administration of justice. The Conference shall seek, with the help of advice from experts as appropriate, measures which would give substantial expression to this aim, considering *inter alia* the possibility of mixed courts in both jurisdictions for the trial of certain offences. The Conference shall also be concerned with policy aspects of extradition and extra-territorial jurisdiction as between North and South.

With regard to cross-border co-operation in security, the Conference was to set in hand a programme of work to be undertaken by the Chief Constable of the RUC and the Commissioner of the Garda Siochana and their officials in such areas as threat assessments, exchange of information, liaison structures, technical co-operation, training of personnel and operational resources. Article 9, which laid this out, also specified that the Conference was to have no operational responsibilities. Article 10 stated that the Governments would co-operate to promote economic and social development in areas which had suffered from the troubles, and should endeavour to secure international support for this work, a coded allusion to the possibility of dollar aid from the United States of America. Article 11 read:

> At the end of three years from signature of this agreement, or earlier if requested by either Government, the working of the conference shall be reviewed by the two Governments to see whether any changes in the scope and nature of its activities are desirable.

The question of an Anglo-Irish parliamentary body was left for consideration by the two parliaments.

The agreement reached at Hillsborough was a remarkable feat of diplomacy. It was a very substantial achievement for two governments, constrained by incompatible commitments from the past, with a history of grievous mutual misunderstanding, to reach such a degree of unanimity of purpose and sensitivity to each other's concerns. It was clear, of course, that the long months of negotiation had failed to produce agreement on a number of major issues: questions such as joint courts, a Bill of Rights, even the Flags and Emblems Act. But instead of allowing these difficulties to stand in the way of an accord being signed, the negotiators had merely transferred these items to the agenda of the intergovernmental conference set up by the agreement. This meant that what was achieved was simply a framework for producing agreed measures, rather than a substantive edifice of agreement. But it was no small thing to produce a definition of the present position of Northern Ireland, a statement of its problems, and a joint mechanism for assisting in their resolution. It was even more remarkable to do so in a way that commanded — as the event was soon to show — the support of the great majority of the populations on each side of the Irish Sea. The whole history of relations between the two islands can hardly show a moment of more warm and genuine accord between a government in Westminster and the representatives of the majority in the island of Ireland.

But despite all this — indeed partly because of all this — the agreement was a triumph which was badly flawed. From the moment of its signing it was obvious, and not only to Unionists and Northern Protestants, that it was badly one-sided. Unionists could claim, with plausibility, that while Hillsborough gave a great deal to nationalists, it gave absolutely nothing to them. They were told that the accord gave an unprecedentedly firm guarantee of their position by the Government of the Republic: but the very skill of the draftsmen had made the first article of the agreement so ambiguous that it was no surprise if it cast suspicions of doublespeak over the entire accord. Unionists were told that as a result of the agreement the Irish Government would increase efforts to root out IRA and INLA terrorism; but that remained to be seen, and in any case they could reply that the Irish Government should already have been doing everything humanly possible in that direction. Finally, it was pointed out to Unionists that the agreement allowed for the influence of the Irish Government to be diminished to the extent that agreement was reached on devolved administration for the province. Unionists could reply that while the agreement thus provided a mechanism to shoehorn than into agreement about devolution, it provided no similar incentives for the SDLP who might well feel better placed with direct access to an equal partner in an intergovernmental conference than with a minority role in a provincial government.

The intrinsic one-sideness of the agreement was aggravated by the way in which it was reached and signed. Given Loyalists' past record of intransigence about the Irish dimension, it was unsurprising that British ministers had not consulted Unionist politicians during the negotiations. Equally, since an agreement subsequently disowned by the SDLP would have been worse than useless to the Irish Government, it was not to be wondered at that John Hume had been taken into their confidence: after all, the negotiations were the outcome of the New Ireland Forum which had been his brainchild. But the official silence in answer to Unionist inquiries was in humiliating contrast with the information given to the SDLP and the frequent leaks in the Irish press.

The bitterness felt by Unionists was eloquently expressed by Harold McCusker in his speech in the House of Commons twelve days later.

> The agreement deals with my most cherished ideals and aspirations. On three occasions in the week prior to the signing of the agreement, on the Tuesday, Wednesday and Thursday, I stood in the House, having been told in essence by foreign journals what the agreement contained, and it was denied to me that an agreement existed, or had even been reached.
>
> I went to Hillsborough on the Friday morning. . . . I stood outside Hillsborough, not waving a Union flag — I doubt whether I will ever wave one again — not singing hymns, saying prayers or protesting, but like a dog and asked the Government to put in my hand the document that sold my birthright. They told me that they would give it to me as soon as possible. Having never consulted me, never sought my opinion or asked my advice, they told the rest of the world what was in store for me.

I stood in the cold outside the gates of Hillsborough castle and waited for them to come out and give me the agreement second hand. It is even more despicable that they could not even send one of their servants to give it to me. I had been told three hours before that it would be brought out to me. At 2.45 pm, 15 minutes after the press conference had begun, I asked a policeman whether he would bring me the declaration that betrayed everything that I had ever stood for. A senior police officer went into Hillsborough castle, asked for the document and brought it out to me.

I felt desolate because as I stood in the cold outside Hillsborough castle everything that I held dear turned to ashes in my mouth.

It is impossible not to be moved by this dignified lament: impossible not to feel that there must have been some more sensitive way in which the agreement could have been communicated, in advance of publication, to Unionist leaders. But the very next words of McCusker's speech show that even justified resentment is a poor guide to perception of reality.

Even in my most pessimistic moments, reading the precise detail in the Irish press on Wednesday before, I never believed that the agreement would deliver me, in the context that it has, into the hands of those who for 15 years have murdered personal friends, political associates, and hundreds of my constituents.

That to describe an agreement whose major purpose, in the eyes of both governments, was to reduce the political influence and the military effectiveness of Sinn Fein and the IRA!

The Sinn Fein leader, Gerry Adams, said that there was nothing in the agreement to make the IRA call off the armed struggle: he described the agreement as a disaster which copper-fastened partition. The Ulster Freedom Fighters, a Protestant paramilitary group linked to the UDA, said that members of the joint conference and secretariat would be legitimate targets. The death threats were condemned by the Rev. Ian Paisley, but he and Mr Molyneaux described the agreement as a 'sell-out' and announced plans to 'derail' it.

A special session of the Assembly on 16 November called for a Northern Ireland referendum on the agreement. If a referendum was refused, the OUP and DUP members of the Westminster Parliament would resign their seats and force a province-wide by-election on the issue. The SDLP rejected a Sinn Fein proposal for an electoral pact which would have enabled Unionists to be ejected from seats with a Catholic voting majority. Unionist Members of Parliament announced a boycott of Northern Ireland ministers, and Unionist members of district councils, and management boards of hospitals, education, health authorities, were called on to absent themselves from meetings. There was an unsuccessful attempt to have the agreement set aside by the High Court in London.

In mainland Britain, initial reaction to the agreement was largely favourable. But Ian Gow, a junior Treasury minister close to Mrs Thatcher, resigned from the Government protesting that the agreement would only prolong the agony of Ulster. In the Republic of Ireland, though Charles Haughey's immediate response was to brand the deal as unconstitutional, opinon was more favourable than had been expected, and this was borne out when the Taisoeach presented the measure to the Dail. Senator Mary Robinson, however, resigned from the Labour party, on the grounds that the agreement was unacceptable to all shades of Unionist opinion. In the North itself, while the SDLP predictably welcomed the agreement, even the Alliance party had serious reservations, but decided, on balance, to support it. On 20 November Tom King was manhandled by a Unionist as he attended a lunch at City Hall, hosted by Unionist mayor John Carson in defiance of the party boycott. On 23 November, a massive Loyalist demonstration in Belfast (its size was estimated by some as 35,000 and by others as 200,000) gave the Unionist MPs an opportunity to pledge to fight the agreement and resign their seats in protest.

17.

The Agreement in the Dail

The debate in the Dail on the Hillsborough agreement was in general a dignified and restrained discussion. In introducing the debate on 19 November, the Taoiseach urged members to avoid remarks that might be divisive or triumphalist. 'Let us above all avoid any word that might endanger the lives of people in Northern Ireland by claiming that any kind of advantage has been obtained through this agreement *vis-à-vis* the Unionist population in Northern Ireland.' He emphasised that the Anglo-Irish process, which had culminated in the agreement, was initiated by the Leader of the Opposition, Mr Haughey, in 1980, and that the first article of the Hillsborough agreement was based on the communiqué issued after the Haughey–Thatcher summit in which the two governments declared that any change in the constitutional status of Northern Ireland would only come about with the consent of a majority of the people of Northern Ireland. This, Dr FitzGerald said, 'provides one of the cornerstones of what has now been agreed, even though the word "constitutional" has been omitted from this phrase in the text of the agreement'.

The role allotted to the Irish Government in the agreement was described as going beyond a consultative role but necessarily, because of the sovereignty issue, falling short of an executive role'. One of the most important sections of the speech spelt out the residual remit of the intergovernmental conference in the event of devolution — a matter on which Mrs Thatcher's statements during the period after the agreement were unclear and not altogether consistent. Dr FitzGerald said:

> It is extremely important to understand that even in the event of devolution the Conference will still have a wide range of functions, concerning matters of particular interest to the Nationalist

minority in Northern Ireland. These include measures to recognise
and to accommodate the rights and identities of the two traditions,
including measures to foster the cultural heritage of both traditions, measures to protect human rights, and to prevent discrimination — changes in electoral arrangements, the use of flags and
emblems, the avoidance of economic and social discrimination and
consideration of the advantages and disadvantages of a Bill of
Rights in Northern Ireland. It will consider the security situation
in Northern Ireland, both addressing policy issues and considering
serious incidents and forthcoming events, including parades and
marches. It will be concerned with the relations between the
security forces and the community, establishing a programme of
special measures to improve these relations, with the object, in
particular, of making the security forces more acceptable to the
Nationalist community.

In the course of his speech Dr FitzGerald was at pains to spell out the
way in which the agreement, and in particular the preamble, echoed the
principles and the wording of the New Ireland Forum, particularly
stressing that the preamble recognised the rights of the two major traditions including 'those who aspire to a sovereign united Ireland achieved
by peaceful means and through agreement'. He pointed out that these
words echoed the third Forum principle which referred to the political
arrangements 'for a new and sovereign Ireland'.

> The incorporation in this agreement of almost the whole corpus of
> the principles set out by the Forum as necessary elements of a
> framework within which a new Ireland could emerge, is a tribute
> to the four constitutional parties which drew up this set of princi-
> ples on a consensus basis.

The Forum, however, had proclaimed the unitary state as its preferred
option, and the Hillsborough agreement was far from this, and indeed
very different from the other models of confederation or joint authority.
The Taoiseach explained:

> The Government adhered loyally to this negotiating brief and it
> was only after exploration of the different models set out in para-
> graphs 5.7 to 5.9, and after it emerged that the British Government

were not prepared to agree to any of these models, that the Government proceeded to seek agreement, on the basis of paragraph 5.10, to proposals that would in some other way accommodate all the necessary elements of the framework proposed by the Forum in paragraph 5.2 of their report.

The main object of the Government, he concluded, was to end the alienation of the minority in Northern Ireland:

> if that alienation can be ended, the terrorists of the IRA whose objective is to maim and murder members of the Unionist community in the hope of bludgeoning them into submission, will suffer such a profound rejection among the minority in Northern Ireland that those terrorists would no longer be able to continue their bloody campaign.

For the opposition, Mr Haughey moved an amendment reaffirming the Forum's preference for a unitary state, and calling for a constitutional conference under the auspices of the two governments 'to formulate new constitutional arrangements which would lead to uniting all the people of Ireland in peace and harmony'. Fianna Fail, he said, was concerned that 'by signing this Agreement the Irish Government are acting in a manner repugnant to the Constitution of Ireland by fully accepting British sovereignty over a part of the national territory and by purporting to give legitimacy to a British administration in Ireland'.

> For the first time the legitimacy of Partition has been recognised by the Republic; the British guarantee to the Unionists has been reinforced by the Irish Government; and the Government are also endorsing the British military and political presence in Ireland. The Irish Government are saying to the world that Northern Ireland is legitimately part of the British State, that Northern Ireland is no longer part of the national territory. An Irish official is actually quoted in *The Sunday Times* as saying 'The RUC has now been legitimised by the agreement between our two Governments'. The absolute sovereignty of the British Government in Northern Ireland has now been conceded.

How would the agreement affect future Irish governments? There is a rule of international law that a state cannot plead its own constitution as a reason for not complying with an international obligation. But there is an exception of what is done is manifestly 'contrary to a rule of its internal law of fundamental importance'. This agreement, Mr Haughey maintained, was clearly of this kind.

> Since neither the Government of the day nor the Oireachtas [Parliament] have any authority to act in conflict with Articles 2 and 3, no future Government need unless it so wishes be bound by the provisions of any international agreement which are incompatible with those of the Constitution.

Mr Haughey went on to confirm the Unionist interpretation of that part of the Forum Report which had proclaimed the necessity of agreement to the arrangements for a new and sovereign Ireland.

> When we speak of the need to secure the agreement of the Unionist population, that agreement applies to the new arrangements for, but not to the concept of, a united Ireland.

Many people, Mr Haughey said, looked on the agreement as a first step towards the unity of Ireland.

> Regrettably, however, it is nothing of the kind. In fact, the whole thrust of the agreement, certainly in so far as Britain is concerned, is in exactly the opposite direction.

Many people in Great Britain and Northern Ireland, if they read Mr Haughey's speech, must have hoped that his assessment of the nature of the agreement was true: that it reinforced partition and gave the Republic of Ireland's blessing to Northern Ireland's institutions. However, the fact that Fianna Fail did not press in the courts any challenge to the constitutionality of the accord suggests that they received legal advice that it was not contrary to articles 2 and 3 of the Constitution. Among those who took this view in the Dail debate was Professor John Kelly, who said he could not read into the agreement an acknowledgement of British sovereignty over Northern Ireland. On the contrary, though it did not go far along the road to Irish unity, it went far enough along it to guarantee that one million people would try to block its success. Not only Mr Haughey, but Gerry Adams also, had rebuked the Irish Government for 'tearing up articles 2 and 3 of the constitution'.

Since when, we may ask, have Sinn Fein and the IRA developed such a tender regard for the Constitution? Have they not themselves repeatedly torn up article 9, which prescribes loyalty to the state as one of the fundamental duties of the citizen? Have they not repeatedly torn up article 15, which describes the Oireachtas as the only legitimate body in the country to maintain an armed force? Have they not torn up article 29 which vests only in the Dail the right to maintain a war? Have they not torn up article 40, which contains the right to live? What about article 41, which proclaims the right of the family, which these sanctimonious butchers have on hundreds of occasions destroyed by robbing wives of their husbands and children of their fathers, bringing grief and desolation into thousands of innocent homes? All this, and we are supposed to take lectures on the constitutional proprieties of articles 2 and 3 from Mr Adams.

Whether or not article 1 of the new agreement acknowledged the legitimacy of the constitutional position North of the border, Professor Kelly went on: 'we do it every day in the way we operate our law'. The existence of exchange control, customs offences, the demarcation of the jurisdiction in criminal law, all recognised the border.

None of us in this House can open a bank account in Portadown or buy a house up there without getting the permission of the Central Bank because it is a different jurisdiction.

The only item in the agreement which did make a difficulty for the Constitution was the provision for mixed courts: it would violate article 34 for justice to be administered in the twenty-six counties by a judge not appointed under the Irish Constitution.

The rest of the Dail debate did not add greatly to the points made in the first three speeches. Fianna Fail deputies emphasised that the agreement might lead the Irish Government to have a share in the responsibility for activities it would find embarrassing: strip-searching, the use of supergrasses, plastic bullets, Diplock courts. The British Government's purpose in the agreement was to muzzle Irish criticism.

The build-up of Irish army resources on the border was an unnecessary expense for the Irish taxpayer. The reference in article 5 and article 8 to measures which might be taken in the Irish Republic after discussion in the Conference was a threat to erode the Republic's state sovereignty. Altogether, the Government had accepted responsibility without power. As Deputy Gallaher put it, 'We have given everything and received nothing in return.'

The Workers' party supported the agreement, but with grave reservations: it was an agreement between two ruling classes which did nothing for workers, Catholic or Protestant: it was an agreement between London and Dublin, not between the Shankill and the Falls. Tomas McGiolla emphasised, 'There has never been such anger and such fear among the Protestant community.' Reluctantly, his party accepted the agreement as the lesser of two evils.

> This agreement can only have meaning if it leads to peace and the beginning of political dialogue in Northern Ireland. If it replaces alienation of Nationalists with alienation of Unionists then the position will be worse than before.

The Labour party, as partner in the ruling coalition, naturally favoured the agreement. The Tanaiste, Dick Spring, insisted that the agreement contained no formal surrender of *de jure* Irish sovereignty over Northern Ireland. On the other hand, he asked deputies, 'Can anyone here imagine what it would be like to live in a united Ireland with one million people in rebellion?' The agreement, he said, went beyond a right to consult or be consulted: he drew attention to article 2(b) which said that determined efforts were to be made through the Conference to resolve any differences. Other members of the Labour party emphasised the need for the South to liberalise its laws, to recognise rights such as the right to divorce, not just in order to achieve harmony with the North, but for its own sake. One member suggested that out of deference to Unionist opinion the Conference should meet not always in Belfast, but sometimes in Dublin and sometimes in London.

The Ministers who spoke after the Taoiseach stressed different aspects of the agreement. Mr Noonan who had visited the United States now described the warmth which the accord had received; he reported on answers he had given to questioning, *inter alia* about the UDR:

I took care to give a balanced answer . . . an answer that reflected in full the many grounds that Nationalists have had for serious complaints against the security forces, and especially the UDR, but an answer that also recognised the fact that the UDR were genuinely regarded by many members of the majority community as providing an essential measure of protection against a ruthless murder campaign. I repeatedly made the point that, in recent times, evidence of even-handed enforcement of the law had been given by the RUC in some situations that were difficult for them.

Mr Peter Barry, summing up for the Government, repeated the point made by the Taoiseach:

whether or not there is devolution, the Intergovernmental conference will continue to deal with human rights, justice, law and order, questions of identity and culture: in other words, all the most difficult and sensitive issues in the North.

The most informative remark about the Government's view of the constitutional issue was made by Mr Desmond, the Minister of Health:

A sizeable portion of the time spent in discussing and revising the draft agreement was concerned with considering the best legal advice from both countries on the legal and constitutional implications of the wording of the agreement. The constitutional cases brought by some Republicans at the time of the Sunningdale agreement were reviewed as well as the British legal position, and the consensus from both countries' legal experts was that the agreement was sound and could not be invalidated on legal grounds.

Mr Desmond quoted favourably a formulation of Professor Kevin Boyle in an article in the *Sunday Independent* of 17 November:

Irish Governments have always behaved internationally on the basis that our supposed claim to Northern Ireland was in reality an aspiration of the *nation* to be united and not an assertion that this *State* claimed Northern Ireland as part of its territory which in some way was illegally occupied by a foreign state. Articles 2 and 3 concern the political theory that the Irish nation should be united some day. They do not represent a claim to the territory of Northern Ireland.

Mr Desmond pointed out that when Fianna Fail signed the treaty of Accession to the European Community in 1973 it accepted that Britain was signing on behalf of the United Kingdom of Great Britain and Northern Ireland: it had not exchanged any notes about the issue, as other member countries had in cases of disputed areas of land.

18.

The Agreement at Westminster

It is instructive to set beside the record of the Dail debates the record of the House of Commons debates a few days later. The Prime Minister and the Leader of the Opposition spoke in rare unison in support of the agreement. Mrs Thatcher insisted that the intergovernmental conference 'will have no executive authority either now or in the future'. She emphasised the difficulties in mixed courts, and welcomed the Irish Government's intention to accede to the European convention on the suppression of terrorism, which would have the effect that offences involving the use of explosives or firearms could not again be regarded as political offences in Ireland. 'The agreement', she said, 'does not set us on some imagined slippery slope to Irish unity, and it is nonsense to claim that it might.'

Mr Kinnock said, having quoted from the Taoiseach's speech in the Dail,

> That is the reward that the gunmen got for their violence. They have engendered such revulsion against insecurity, fear and brutality that they have made Nationalists seek change even at the cost of indefinitely postponing their own Nationalist aspirations.

Mr Ian Gow, in a moving speech explaining the reasons for his resignation, took precisely the opposite view:

> Our fellow countrymen from Northern Ireland will perceive — and will not be wrong in perceiving — that the agreement would never have been signed unless there had been a prolonged campaign of violence. The agreement will be perceived as having been won as a result of violence. The Irish National Liberation Army and the Irish Republican Army will believe that their violence is succeeding.

113

One after another the Unionist MPs rose to express their anger, their sense of betrayal, and their fears for the future of the province. Peter Robinson affirmed, 'The agreement is intended to trundle Northern Ireland into an all-Ireland Republic.' He insisted that the agreement was more than consultative, and quoted a description of it by the Dean of the Faculty of Law at University College, Cork. Northern Ireland

> . . . is a province of the United Kingdom which for the first time has become subject to the legal rights of two sovereign governments to determine how all matters which go to the heart of sovereignty in that area shall in future be determined.

Ken Maginnis, representing a border constituency, felt particularly strongly about the role given the Republic about security and related matters.

> That means that another Government are being given an opportunity to deal with a reserved matter — a right that will be denied to British citizens living in Northern Ireland even if they are members of a devolved administration.

The Rev. Ian Paisley, too, was worried about the conference being given a security role: it meant, he believed, that information would be leaked to terrorists. But what worried him most about the conference was this:

> The conference is not between Ministers of the South and Ministers of the North but three ways, between the Republic, the SDLP and Northern Ireland Ministers. That meant that the SDLP can go to see Ministers as public representatives, come to the Assembly if they want to — they do not come — and best of all they have the ear of the Dublin Government, through which they can put their views.

Despite his opposition to the agreements, he did not wish to take Ulster out of the United Kingdom. He had not observed any blooming of Ulster nationalism, and he had no time for UDI.

Mr Paisley found the most worrying part of the agreement article 3, providing for a United Ireland if the majority wished for it.

> We are told that the House wishes to safeguard the minority, but

what if the minority changes? I was told by a man today 'You will be bred out anyway in 20 years.' I heard that when I was a boy of 12 and they are still breeding us out. But it is interesting to remember that Roman Catholic Unionists also breed. I say nothing about the virility of the Protestants. There is no safeguard here for the minority. If the population is 49.9 per cent Protestant and the remainder is Roman Catholic or Nationalist, the Government will seek to establish a united Ireland.

Other Unionist members wondered what value could be placed on the Irish Government's guarantee of the Unionist position in the meantime. Harold McCusker reminded the House that a binding agreement had been signed in 1925 by Baldwin, Cosgrave, O'Higgins and Craig, and registered with the League of Nations.

That agreement recognised the legitimacy of the state of Northern Ireland. It recognised the international frontier of Northern Ireland. Of course, five or six years later, De Valera said that it was extracted under duress. That was about four years after he had had Kevin O'Higgins murdered, who, after he had signed that agreement, described it as the best day's work that he had ever done for Ireland.

Senior statesmen of both parties, such as Edward Heath, James Prior, Humphrey Atkins, Roy Mason, added their weight to the support of both front benches for the agreement. Opposition came from the right wing of the Conservative party and from the left wing of the Labour party. Mr Ivor Stanbrook thought that offering a special role to a foreign government set a disastrous precedent. Jamaica and India would now have a precedent for demanding a right to be consulted about the grievances of their citizens in the United Kingdom. The agreement, he said,

> is a bad agreement, conceived in desperation, born out of fear of violence and foreign pressure, and confirmed in folly. It will make matters worse, not better, in Northern Ireland.

Miss Joan Maynard and a number of Labour supporters, including Mr Tony Benn, voted against the agreement because it fell short of a

United Ireland. Miss Maynard, quoting a *Mirror* leader, said that Mrs Thatcher and all party leaders of both parties in the past

> have failed because they refuse to recognise the heart of the problem, which is the British presence in Ireland. We will not take the first step to peace until that is removed.

If a referendum was held of the whole United Kingdom, there would be a massive vote in support of withdrawal.

Alliance speakers supported the accord. Dr David Owen called for a Bill of Rights; in addition, an interparliamentary tier, and proportional representation for the Northern Ireland parliamentary seats. David Alton, welcoming the agreement, pressed the SDLP to return to the Assembly and to encourage Catholics to join the RUC. John Hume, commending the agreement with his customary eloquence, said in response:

> I want the people whom I represent to play the fullest part, as to any citizens in a democratic society, in the process of peace and order. While we await the outcome we shall continue to give our full and unqualified support to the police force in impartially seeking out anybody who commits a crime in Northern Ireland.

Peter Robinson had quoted him as saying, in an RTE interview, 'We are not waiting for Irish unity. We are working for it.' Hume retorted, 'I went on to say that those who think that Irish unity is round the corner are wired to the moon.'

One of the most striking speeches in the debate came from Mr Enoch Powell. He made a constitutional point which has often since been echoed by Unionists to justify opposition to the agreement. Law in the United Kingdom is made not by the House of Commons, but by the Queen in Parliament.

> It is not true to say that if the motion that is before the House is carried tonight the law of the United Kingdom will have been altered. All that will have happened will be that approval has been given, perhaps by a majority, to the action of the Government in entering into an external contract. . . . But no one will be able to say after the Division tonight that the people of Northern Ireland are under an obligation to accept — whatever might be the

meaning of the term 'accept' in that context — the Anglo-Irish agreement that has been made between the two Prime Ministers.

Anyone watching the Prime Minister at Hillsborough, he said, would see that 'here was someone doing what she knew was wrong and what she knew was contrary to her instincts and knowledge of the position'. What force had made her do it? It was done because the United States insisted it should be done. The agreement was the price the Irish Government had exacted for collaboration with NATO.

At the end of the two-day debate, the motion approving the agreement was carried by 473 votes to 47: one of the largest majorities on a division in Parliamentary history.

19.

Six Months after Hillsborough

On 2 December the RUC Chief Constable, Sir John Hermon, met Commissioner Wren of the Republic's Garda at Dublin. It was their first meeting for almost three years, and was intended to symbolise the increased co-operation on security which was to be introduced following Hillsborough. On the following day in Brussels, at a business luncheon, the Northern Ireland Secretary Tom King said that the agreement showed that the Irish Prime Minister 'has in fact accepted that for all practical purposes and into perpetuity there will never be a united Ireland'. On 17 December, in an interview with the *Belfast Telegraph*, Mrs Thatcher told Unionists that they could end the Anglo-Irish governmental conference by reaching agreement on devolved government for Northern Ireland. Both these statements may have been true as a matter of practical politics, but they contrasted with the carefully worded terms of the agreement and the residual role allocated to Dublin after any devolution.

The first session of the Anglo-Irish conference was held on Wednesday, 11 December at Stormont Castle, protected from enraged Unionist demonstrators by rolls of barbed wire and hundreds of police. During the session, workers at Harland and Wolff Shipyard marched out at lunchtime to the Anglo-Irish secretariat at Maryfield, and some were involved in scuffles with the RUC. The outcome of the conference was that a code of conduct for the RUC was promised, in order to re-assure Northern Catholics, and extra forces from the Republic were to be devoted to the border area to improve security.

On 18 December one of the largest of the 'supergrass' trials came to an end: twenty-five of twenty-seven defendants in an INLA case were convicted on the uncorroborated evidence of Harry Kirkpatrick. On the following day one of the convicted began to hunger strike in the

Maze prison. The hunger strike and the system of supergrass trials were on the agenda at a special meeting of the Anglo-Irish conference in London on 30 December. Two other prisoners joined the strike, but it ended soon after. The year ended with a march from Derry to Maryfield, organised by the youth branches of the OUP and DUP, which reached Maryfield on 4 January, where the gates of the secretariat were torn down amid scuffles. Official Unionists dissociated themselves from the violence, but Peter Robinson, the deputy leader of the DUP, refused to condemn it. The Republican paramilitaries marked the beginning of the new year by killing two members of the RUC by remote controlled bomb minutes after midnight. In a dawn raid on 28 December eighteen Sinn Fein members had been arrested: Sinn Fein president Gerry Adams claimed that the SDLP and the Government of the Republic were reponsible for the arrests.

The third meeting of the Anglo-Irish conference took place on 10 January in London: the Irish Foreign Minister and Minister for Justice met Tom King and Nick Scott, with the police chiefs in attendance. According to the communiqué the Ministers discussed the administration of justice, police co-operation and the police complaints system in Northern Ireland; extradition; the Flags and Emblems Act; and the status of the Irish language in Northern Ireland. It was announced that the attorney generals of the two states would meet in February to discuss the administration of justice, in particular uncorroborated informer evidence and the Diplock courts. It was announced that UDR patrols were to be accompanied everywhere by the RUC, and act in their support: relationships with civilians were to be carried out exclusively by the police. On the next day Unionist members of Belfast City Council erected a 40-foot banner outside City Hall proclaiming 'Belfast Says NO'.

The by-elections caused by the resignation of the fifteen Unionist Members of Parliament were held on 23 January. Unionist candidates received 418,230 votes — short of the half-million they had aimed at, but enough to enable them to claim that they had received a massive endorsement of their opposition to the Hillsborough agreement. On the other hand, they lost the seat in Newry and Armagh, where Seamus Mallon, the deputy leader of the SDLP, was elected with a majority of 2583, thus doubling SDLP representation at Westminster. Moreover, in the four constituencies where both the SDLP and SF were fielding candidates, the Sinn Fein share of the nationalist vote fell from 41.9 to 35.4 per cent. Thus politicians in the Republic of Ireland could claim that progress had been made in achieving one of the goals of the agreement, namely winning Catholics back from their support of Sinn Fein and strengthening the hand of constitutional nationalism. The fact remained that overall 78.1 per cent of the votes cast were for parties (whether Unionist or Sinn Fein) opposing the agreement, and only 21.9 per cent for candidates favouring the agreement (including the dummy candidates, all bearing the name 'Peter Barry', who had been put up by Unionists in order to ensure that a vote was taken in otherwise uncontested constituencies).

Before the election, Unionist politicians from the two parties presented a united front of opposition to the agreement. Once the election was over, there was a greater uncertainty about the political tactics to be adopted for the future. The two deputy leaders, Harold McCusker and Peter Robinson, announced on 26 January that they would sign the book at Westminster, but they would not take their seats: it would be difficult, they said, to sustain a Unionist boycott of local government if MPs were not boycotting the Westminster Parliament.

In the aftermath of Hillsborough, a new organisation came into prominence: the Ulster Clubs, originally formed to oppose the rerouting of marches in 1985. Its leader, Alan Wright, described its goals as 'The right to self-determination for the Ulster people, to maintain the Union as long as it's in our best interest, to combat the encroachment of Irish nationalism, and to unify the talents, abilities, and resources at our disposal.' It was not clear whether the 'resources' included military means. Wright denied that the Ulster Clubs was a paramilitary organisation, but said, 'Ultimately, because my faith, my province and my children matter, if violence is the only way that I can uphold these things then I will, while not being a violent man, resort to force.' The Ulster Clubs called on the fourteen Unionist MPs to pull out of Westminster and give decisive leadership.

At the end of January Harold McCusker called for a tripartite conference of British, Irish and Northern Irish politicians to discuss 'the totality of relationships' in the two islands. This suggestion was welcomed by Fianna Fail in the Republic, and endorsed by Peter Robinson. It evoked no response from the British Government, other than an invitation on 4 February from the Prime Minister to the Unionist leaders to have talks on the Anglo-Irish agreement. Dr FitzGerald, in a radio programme, while insisting the agreement would not be scrapped, said that he did not rule out talks on a tripartite basis.

It was not only the Fine-Gael-Labour coalition and the Fianna Fail opposition whose opinions now counted in politics in the Republic. A new party had been formed, the Progressive Democrats, led by Desmond O'Malley, a long-standing opponent of Mr Haughey in the Fianna Fail party, pledged to breaking the mould of Irish politics formed in the aftermath of the civil war. Within eight weeks of its foundation the party could claim 14,000 members, and was the fourth largest party in the Dail; in February an opinion poll gave it 25 per cent of first preference votes, more than those for Dr FitzGerald's own party. And while both parties were overshadowed in opinion polls by Fianna Fail, with 42 per cent of the votes, the emergence of the PD can only serve to strengthen the position of the Anglo-Irish agreement. For it now appears unlikely that Fianna Fail would emerge from the next election with an overall majority, and whatever coalition forms the next Irish Government is unlikely to be led by Mr Haughey.

In Belfast, on a case taken by the Alliance party, the High Court ordered the removal of the 'Belfast says NO' banner, and told the Council to resume normal business. The eighteen Unionist-controlled councils had refused to strike a rate; on 14 February they were granted an extension of the deadline by the Northern Ireland Court of Appeal. John Carson, the Lord Mayor of Belfast, tried in vain to persuade his Unionist colleagues to hold a meeting to strike a rate.

On 25 February Unionist leaders Paisley and Molyneaux met Mrs Thatcher at Downing St. On the eve of the meeting Molyneaux had said that he would ask for a three-month suspension of the agreement, and indicated that Unionists would consider talks if given an equal voice with Dublin. After the meeting, at which Mrs Thatcher promised to implement the agreement 'sensitively' and to consider favourably the Unionist proposals for round table talks on devolution, Molyneaux spoke of a breaking of a deadlock, and King said 'there is a real opportunity to make a new start in Northern Ireland after years and years of stalemate'.

Four principal issues were raised at the meetings. Mrs Thatcher said that the Government would like to establish new arrangements for enabling Unionists to make their views known to the Government on the province's affairs; she offered consultations about the future of the Northern Ireland Assembly and about arrangements for handling the province's business at Westminster. She also agreed to consider a round table conference to discuss devolved government, and she said that if progress was made 'we should need to consider what that meant for the work of the intergovernmental conference set up under the terms of the Anglo-Irish agreement'.

The euphoria which this meeting engendered was very short-lived. After the Unionist leaders returned to Belfast and met other Unionists and workers from shipyards and power stations they announced that they would hold no further talks with the Prime Minister unless the Anglo-Irish deal was scrapped: they were, they said, 'withdrawing consent from the Government'. In a debate in the Assembly the following day they announced a 24-hour general strike for 3 March: it was to be a voluntary and peaceful protest.

The strike was organised by a committee of shop stewards, known as 'the 1986 workers committee', linked to a number of DUP politicians. The measures taken went far beyond those officially blessed by the political leaders. Members of the Ulster Clubs threatened a permanent boycott of any shops or factories which stayed open. Schools were closed, public services disrupted, electricity cuts forced, roadblocks set up, and public transport largely interrupted. Some areas were sealed off by barricades manned by masked bravos. A factory in Lurgan was besieged by a mob and destroyed by petrol bombs. Shots were fired at the RUC in Protestant areas of Belfast. The RUC and NIO were widely criticised for failing to keep the roads clear, though they had removed 441 out of 665, and 47 policemen had been injured during the day. Sir John Hermon felt it necessary to speak on Irish RTE to defend the RUC against charges that they had failed to prevent intimidation, and had condoned Loyalist barricading. He admitted that the police had not always had sufficient strength to deal with particular situations, but pointed out that fifteen members of the RUC had been forced to leave their homes with their families, as a result of Loyalist attacks upon them.

Since Hillsborough, the position of the police had indeed been very difficult. 1985 had seen many well-organised attacks on the police by Republican paramilitaries. The Ulsterisation policy of 1976, which had placed the police, rather than the army, in the front line of the battle against terrorism, and the increasing professionalism of the PIRA with its new concentration on narrowly defined 'legitimate targets', had combined together to make 1985 the worst year for police deaths for ten years. Twenty-three officers were killed in 1985 in addition to the two in the first minutes of the new year of 1986. But after Hillsborough the RUC had to fight on two fronts, and by February more than 100 policemen had been injured in clashes with Loyalists.

The RUC is a predominantly Protestant force: in January 1986 only 1100 members of the 11,014 full-time and reserve members were Catholic. Under Sir John Hermon's leadership it had established a reputation, even among Catholics, for a professional even-handedness between the two communities. But however non-political the force's public stance, many of its members must have been disconcerted by the Anglo-Irish agreement, and some of them expressed this opposition within the Police Federation in a session later made public on tape by a DUP politician. On 4 February Sir John ordered leaders of the Police Federation not to talk to the media without first obtaining clearance from police headquarters. He has always maintained that the RUC should have no political stance. 'The surest safeguard of the integrity of our position as a police force is our own professionalism, by which I mean simply decent, honest, fair policing.' In March, Molyneaux and Paisley suggested that the role of RUC officers under the Anglo-Irish agreement would be contrary to their oath of allegiance to the Crown. The Northern Ireland Police authority blamed the Unionist leaders for trying to exert political influence over the RUC and insisted that it was not the purpose of the police to attack or defend the Hillsborough agreement.

Attacks on the homes of police families continued. Violence between police and Loyalists came to a head on 31 March after the banning of the march of the Apprentice Boys of Derry in Portadown on that day: 39 policemen and 38 civilians were injured. The police were praised for their actions by John Hume, and Molyneaux deplored the attacks by Loyalists. But Peter Robinson, regretting the incidents, refused to condemn them; and on the night of 4 April alone fourteen RUC members' homes were attacked. It was only after the Rev. Ian Paisley cut short a visit to America to condemn the attacks unequivocally that the number of such incidents diminished.

The fourth meeting of the Anglo-Irish ministerial conference, originally announced for February, was held at Stormont on 11 March, amid security and demonstrations which were a minor replay of the first Stormont conference. The meeting dealt with cross-border security and co-operation in economic and social spheres; the Irish delegation put forward views on behalf of the minority in relation to education, health and housing. Little substantial progress seems to have been made, and in the Republic of Ireland there were signs of impatience that the conference had not yet achieved even the repeal of the Flags and Emblems Act. On the same day, in Washington, the House of Representatives agreed unanimously on a five-year aid package, worth $250,000,000, for Northern Ireland to symbolise American support for the accord. The vote did not impress Unionists, who threw pieces of silver at the police outside Stormont, classing them as Judases who had sold out to a foreign power for sordid financial gain. Five hundred and fifty extra troops were moved to Northern Ireland from the mainland, bringing the level to the highest for three years.

The cause of Anglo-Irish co-operation in law enforcement suffered an unexpected and unnecessary setback at the end of March. Evelyn Glenholmes was a woman wanted on charges of terrorist offences in the United Kingdom committed between 1981 and 1982. In 1984 warrants were sent to Ireland for her extradition; they contained technical errors, which the Irish authorities pointed out; by the time the errors had been corrected she had disappeared. She was arrested in Dublin on 12 March, and the extradition hearings reopened in the Irish courts on the basis of the second set of warrants. These were found invalid by the Dublin district court on 22 March. Glenholmes was released; the British authorities prepared fresh warrants, and she was rearrested, and once again released by the District Court, on the grounds that there was insufficient evidence that the new warrants were ready. By the time the fresh warrants reached Dublin on 25 March, Glenholmes had once more vanished into hiding. Home Secretary Douglas Hurd had to tell the Commons that the Irish authorities had

behaved correctly, and that the fault lay with the British Director
of Public Prosecutions. In the angry debate which followed, the most
telling remark was that of Sir Eldon Griffiths. 'There is a painful
contrast between the detailed and careful and often dangerous work of
the police service of the Irish Republic and the Metropolitan Police and
the RUC in undertaking to obtain the information, sometimes at the
risk of their lives, and the slipshod and careless way in which that was
dealt with within the DPP's office.'

There were some, of course, especially among Unionists, who
thought that the Dublin court was too ready to take refuge in a techni-
cality to release a suspected terrorist. But the Glenholmes case was not
the first but the fourth case to end in a débacle since the decisions of the
Irish courts in the cases of McGlinchey and Shannon first allowed the
extradition of IRA suspects. Dominic McGlinchey, found guilty by a
Belfast court after extradition for the murder of an elderly postmistress
in 1977, was later acquitted on Appeal; he had to be re-extradited to the
South, where he was jailed for ten years for shooting at the Garda while
resisting arrest. Seamus Shannon, the second extraditee, was acquitted
at Belfast Crown Court in December 1985 of the charge of murdering a
former Stormont speaker and his son in 1981. In the same month, an
application was made to a Dublin court for the extradition of Brendan
Burns, wanted for the murder of five British soldiers in the North. But
he walked free from the Court because the extradition warrants issued
by the RUC were quashed in Belfast by the Chief Justice of Northern
Ireland. In all these cases there can be no question of the co-
operativeness of the Irish authorities or the impartiality of the Northern
judiciary: it was, as in the Glenholmes case, the prosecuting authorities
who had the responsibility for the failure of the prosecution.

In April Mrs Thatcher and Tom King met two Unionist elder
statesmen, Lord Moyola (Ulster Prime Minister as James Chichester-
Clark) and Lord Brookeborough (a member of the last Stormont
Government). This led to rumours that some concession to Unionists
was imminent; but the Government and the Opposition at once
reaffirmed bipartisan support for the Anglo-Irish agreement.
'The Government is committed', said Mrs Thatcher, 'to the Anglo-
Irish accord and to its implementation and will continue to implement
it.' She renewed her call to Unionists to meet to continue discussion of

the four issues identified at the 25 February meeting; but Mr Molyneaux said that talks 'could not be tolerated' against the background of the Hillsborough agreement.

Loyalist violence flared up again at the funeral of Kevin White, a twenty-year-old man who had been fatally wounded by a plastic bullet during the Portadown rioting on Easter Monday. He was the first Protestant to die from a police plastic bullet, and the first fatality as a result of the protests against the Hillsborough accord. Despite appeals for calm from Unionist politicians, Loyalist youths rioted in Belfast through the night. They erected barricades, attacked police with stones, guns and bombs, and caused a million pounds worth of damage. The police later siezed arms and ammunition from Loyalist centres. Next day there was further rioting in Portadown.

By now the Unionist political leaders were clearly alarmed at the danger of disturbances beyond their control. The Assembly met in special session on 23 April to announce a programme of protest and civil disobedience, in the hope of seizing the political initiative back from the paramilitaries. A twelve-point package of measures was approved, including the withholding of rates payments and a day of prayer for 'deliverance' from the agreement.

As the sixth month from the signing of the agreement expired, the province waited uneasily for the summer marching season. The first of the season, a march planned at Portadown on 5 May to protest over the banning of the Easter Sunday march, was cancelled at the persuasion of Ulster politicians, including Mr Ian Paisley, who were thereupon described as 'gutless' by the Ulster Clubs.

Sir John Hermon openly attacked the sectarianism of the Loyalist ascendancy and the speeches of Northern Ireland politicians which amounted to incitement to mutiny. This was in response to one of the Assembly's twelve points, which was 'further to urge the officers of the RUC to act on the already expressed and growing reluctance of their members in policing an agreement that does not have community support'. Trying in this way to create disaffection within the RUC, said Hermon, 'is bordering on subversive behaviour by these people, if not legally beyond any doubt, then morally'.

In the six months since Hillsborough 300 attacks had been made on police on duty, 300 attacks on their homes, and 50 police had had to be rehoused. During the months which remain before Hillsborough is a year old, there are 1800 parades to be handled by the police. Some of these involve Protestant marches through Catholic areas: flaunting of ascendancy in areas where the population balance has changed. It is these which are the most sensitive to handle. Hermon suggested in place of the present rules, where the RUC has the decision whether to permit the march, or reroute it, or ask the Secretary of State to ban it, that notice of a contentious parade should go to an independent tribunal, before which the police, organisers and local people could each present their case.

As the summer marching season of 1986 approached it was clear that the RUC were due for a difficult task in policing Protestant marches and enforcing reroutings away from areas where they might be found provocative. But in June a bizarre turn of events called into question once again the integrity of the force in its dealings with the Catholic minority on the other side. This was the suspension of Mr John Stalker, deputy chief constable of Greater Manchester, who had been conducting an inquiry into an alleged shoot-to-kill policy by the RUC.

During the autumn of 1982 five unarmed Republicans and a nationalist youth were shot dead in three separate shooting incidents by an undercover surveillance group of RUC officers specially trained and specially armed. Nationalist leaders claimed that the killings had been deliberate acts of policy; RUC officers accused of the murders were all later acquitted. An inquiry into the events was set up under Mr Stalker, and sixteen months was spent investigating the operations of RUC undercover officers. In September 1985 he presented an interim report to Sir John Hermon, which is believed to have been highly critical of aspects of the RUC's anti-terrorist activity. Four days before he was due to fly to Belfast for the final stage of his inquiries into the allegations of the shoot-to-kill policy, Mr Stalker was suspended after disciplinary allegations concerning compromising friendships. Inevitably, suggestions were made that the allegations originated from people who were anxious to delay the publication of his report and to discredit it in advance.

In June 1986 the Cabinet decided to dissolve the Northern Ireland Assembly. Its legal basis was not abolished, but it was decided to hold no further elections when the present Assembly reached the end of its normal life in October. The date of elections for a new Assembly was left open. Since the Hillsborough agreement the Assembly, now boycotted by all except the two Unionist parties, had ceased to carry out any of its statutory functions of scrutinising Westminster legislation and making proposals for devolution.

After Hillsborough, many admirers of Dr FitzGerald hoped that he would propose a referendum on the abolition of articles 2 and 3 of the Irish Constitution: the popularity of the accord among Irish voters gave good hope of success, and the abolition would be the best possible pledge of good faith to the Northern Protestants. Instead, Dr FitzGerald proposed a referendum to remove the constitutional ban on divorce. There was strong pressure in the Republic, for internal reasons, for such a reform; but the Taoiseach also urged that it would improve relations with the North. Though in advance of the referendum opinion polls had predicted a substantial majority in favour of reform, the eventual vote was 'No' by a majority of more than three to two.

Paradoxically, the defeat of the referendum may have done something to reconcile Protestants in the North to the agreement, by making it seem much less likely that a United Ireland was lurking in the wings. Such at least seems to have been the attitude of Dr Paisley. When escorted from the Assembly chamber after its dissolution, he proclaimed loudly that Northern Ireland was on the verge of civil war. Seven days later he announced that the threat had receded — it had indeed been disowned by the largest paramilitary organisation, the UDF — because the divorce referendum had brought the country 'back from the brink'.

20.

After the Marching Season

Eight months after the signing of the agreement at Hillsborough neither the fears of its critics nor the hopes of its supporters have been realised. Those who predicted that the Unionist reaction would be so hostile that the province would rapidly become ungovernable have been proved wrong: the Hillsborough accord has already lasted longer than the Sunningdale agreement. Those who hoped for a speedy end to violence, and a new era of peace and stability, have not yet seen their hopes fulfilled. Unionist dislike of the agreement has been so strong and so widespread that neither Government has dared to make any of the reforms which Nationalists may have looked for: not even the Flags and Emblems Act has been repealed, and justice continues to be dispensed through Diplock courts.

There is no doubt that the Hillsborough agreement was one-sided: if it can be seen to have given, so far, rather little to the Nationalists in concrete terms, it gave them a great deal in terms of symbols. To the Unionists, it has so far offered nothing but humiliation: some have even said that the only thing it has given to the Nationalists has been the pleasure of seeing Unionist disarray. However exaggerated the Unionist reaction has been, however absurd the comparisons with Munich and Hungary, the Unionists have one unanswerable argument against the agreement — an argument which has been consistently used against them by British ministers in past years. A province cannot be given just and stable government if the political institutions are not accepted by a substantial portion of the population. If this is true when the discontented are in a minority, it is doubly true when they are in a majority.

But to say that the Hillsborough agreement was one-sided is not to say that it ought to be put aside. It is not even to say that it was a mistake. On the contrary, it was a great achievement: but it is incomplete. One-sided movements and actions are a normal part of human affairs. Whether they are steering cars, sailing boats, or driving golf balls, human beings progress by making adjustments, first in one direction, then in another; by making corrections and then further correction to compensate for overcorrection.

Even those who are most critical of the Hillsborough agreement commonly accept that to set it aside would be a catastrophe. The unanimity between the two sovereign governments is a precious thing, painfully achieved: without it there can be no hope of permanent peace in Ireland. Any abandonment of the agreement would be seen as a sign of weakness by paramilitaries in both the Catholic and Protestant camps: it would reinforce signals given too often in the past that the threat of violence is the most effective way to influence Government policy. But even if, in the worst case, the Hillsborough agreement were to be brought down, it would have achieved, irreversibly, something of historic significance. It has shown the world that the problem of Northern Ireland is not caused by the presence of British administrators and British soldiers. No one who has followed events since Hillsborough can believe that the province's troubles would end by a simple withdrawal of British power. 'Brits out' is no solution, unless it means the forcible transfer of the entire Protestant population. Paradoxically, the principal effect of Hillsborough may have been to draw the attention of the world to the existence of one million Protestants in Ulster.

That is the message of Hillsborough for the wider world: within the United Kingdom its message has been to emphasise the divide which separates the inhabitants of the province from the inhabitants of the mainland. Before Hillsborough, one of the options most favoured among Unionist politicians was integration: the proposal that the province should be treated in exactly the same way as any other region of the United Kingdom of similar size, such as Yorkshire. This was advocated not only by Conservative politicians in the Unionist camp, such as Mr Enoch Powell, but also by a number of left-wing groups, such as the Campaign for Labour Representation in Northern Ireland. Integration would involve the reorganisation of the present political groupings: the mainland parties would have to permit Northern Ireland members and set up candidates in the province's constituencies; in that way it was hoped that sectarian politics might be superseded. Integrationism was given a fillip by an extempore remark of the Prime Minister's that Ulster was as British as Finchley. The Prime Minister's more considered gesture in signing the Hillsborough accord has surely put an end to the fantasy of integrationism. No one thinks that a non-British Government should have a direct input to local policy decisions in Finchley. By supporting Hillsborough in such overwhelming strength, politicians in Westminster and voters on the Clapham omnibus have shown that they think it perfectly appropriate for the United Kingdom citizens who live in Ulster to be treated quite differently from those who live in England and Scotland and Wales. And, given the history of the province, they are right to think so. That is why the message of Hillsborough was so painful to Unionists: it was a massive affirmation by their fellow citizens that they regard them as a group apart.

If Hillsborough itself underlined the differences between Ulster and Britain, the aftermath of Hillsborough has reinforced the message. To the mainlander, the hostility of the Unionists has seemed to justify their reputation for intransigence, bellicosity and bigotry. To the Ulster Protestant, the incomprehension of their grievances shown by the mainlanders adds insult to perfidy. Each unruly demonstration, every day of boycott, makes the possibility of the integration of Northern Ireland recede further into the past.

Serious and violent resistance to the agreement, of course, calls in question not only integration but the very Union itself. It is quite wrong to think that the agreement was designed to push Ulster into a united Ireland: both Prime Ministers believed that the most likely hope of peace for Northern Ireland, in the foreseeable future, lay under British sovereignty. It is unfortunate that the wish of the British Government to keep Northern Ireland within the United Kingdom was not spelt out in the agreement in the same explicit form as its willingness to agree to a united Ireland if the province's population should opt for that. But there is no reason to doubt that Mrs Thatcher meant what she said when she described herself as a Unionist: that is, as someone who wishes to see Northern Ireland within the United Kingdom. But if the opinion polls are a safe guide, Mrs Thatcher and her fellow-Unionists are in a minority on the mainland of Great Britain. Like Mrs Thatcher, I believe that it is very much to be desired that Northern Ireland should remain within the Union. But the effect of Unionist protest, especially if it escalates during the marching season, will not be to reinforce the Union nor to lead in the direction of a united Ireland, but to take the province towards independence.

From time to time in the past proposals have been aired for setting up an independent Northern Ireland. The most fully-thought-out scheme for negotiated independence was prepared in the late 1970s by the Ulster Political Research Group, an offshoot of the Unionist para-military Ulster Defence Association. In a booklet *Beyond the Religious Divide*, published in 1979, the group proposed an American-style con-stitution for an independent Ulster, based on the principle of the separation of powers and with a system of checks and balances. The executive branch of government would consist of a chief executive and his deputy, who would stand for election like an American President and Vice-President and appoint ministers from outside the legislature. The legislature, elected as a single chamber in multi-member constitu-encies by single transferable vote, would itself elect, by a two-thirds vote, a Speaker who would play a key role. He would appoint the committees of the house, and their chairmen, in proportion to their party strength. Another key figure would be the President of the Supreme Court who would head the judiciary, a figure chosen to be acceptable to both Northern Ireland communities, and appointed to head the Court for the first dozen years of its existence. He would also head a judicial commission, which would include representatives also of industry, trade unions, the law society and the police authority; this commission would appoint the judges and officers of the Supreme Court, the county courts, and the district and inferior courts. An entrenched Bill of Rights would protect individual and communal rights; it would be enforced not only by the Supreme Court, but, at first instance, by a Constitutional Preliminary Hearing Agency, which would investigate allegations against custodians of law and order.

A number of merits were claimed for the scheme of negotiated independence. It would recognise for the first time the reality that both Britain and the Republic of Ireland regard Northern Ireland as a place apart. The major responsibility for resolving the conflicts of the province would shift to the people most involved: without the pull of London and Dublin, all parties would have to get round a table together in Belfast to work out how to live in harmony with each other. Each side would have to forfeit something: nationalists would have to give up their aspiration to a united Ireland, but Unionists would have to give up their allegiance to the British Crown. On the other hand, each side would have gained a cherished objective: Nationalists would have secured British withdrawal, Unionists would be secured against a united Ireland. Because the population balance might well change, producing a Catholic majority in the future, the Protestants would have an interest in a constitution that would provide really firm guarantees to a minority against oppression by a majority.

Beyond the Religious Divide contains some impressive constitutional planning. Mindful of the role played by folklore in the creation of a national identity during the struggle for independence which led to the Republic of Ireland, some of those involved with the UPRG assembled books recalling the legends of the ancient kingdom of Ulster in the centuries before the sectarian divide. Economists, from both North and South of Ireland, were invited to opine on the financial prospects of an independent Ulster. Senator T. K. Whitaker, once a Governor of the Central Bank of Ireland, claimed that 'economic viability, without serious diminution of standards, is possible for an independent Ireland on certain assumptions'.

But whatever the merits of an independent Ulster achieved by negotiation, a statelet constituted by a unilateral declaration of independence would be very different. Catholics would be bound to resist remaining, as a minority, in a political unit which offered them at best nothing different from the Stormont of the 1920s. If the British and Irish Governments felt obliged to use force to prevent the UDI, a bloody and confused struggle would result. More likely, a British government, its electorate's patience with the province's problems exhausted, would withdraw under the best available colour of decency. If an independent Ulster emerged as a result of the ensuing internal strife, it would be likely to be a much smaller state than the six-county state. Repartition, the option rejected as unthinkable by almost everyone who has studied what it would mean on the ground, or even in the atlas, would be enforced in the worst possible of manners. Repartition would involve, at best, massive transfers of Catholic population westward across the Bann, and massive transfers of Protestant populations eastward across the Bann: for, as a glance at the map shows, the two communities are mixed in almost every local government region, however much one religion or the other may predominate in larger areas. At worst, repartition might involve massacres of enclaves left behind — of Protestants in Derry, and Catholics in West Belfast. Once sectarian attacks became frequent, the Irish Government — whether or not the British withdrew — might well feel they could not stand idly by, and a civil war might engulf not only the province, but the entire island.

Fortunately, the dangers awaiting any declaration of independence, against the wishes of the minority in the North and the two sovereign Governments, are very well known to the leaders of the Protestant community. And if we let our imagination dwell on the horrors of the worst case, we must remember that in the first months after Hillsborough not a single life has been taken by those who have protested against it, great though their anger has been.

If integration and independence are both impossible options for Northern Ireland, the solution must be to accept the basis of the agreement, and to build upon it rather than tear it down. Its one-sidedness must be rectified, not by taking away what has been given to the Nationalists, but by giving back to Unionists a proper share in the government of the province which they share with the Catholics. What is offered to the Unionists must be something which is not against the agreement but within the agreement or around the agreement. Within the agreement there is ample scope for devolution: the scope could be extended, even into security matters, when the agreement comes up for review, provided that in the mean time there has been some experience of successful devolved government in less contentious areas. Around the agreement there could be set up tripartite structures of the sort for which Unionists have, in recent months, been asking: a structure within which the elected representatives of the people of Northern Ireland could talk on equal terms with the two Governments whose concerns and responsibilities are enshrined in Hillsborough.

Devolved government in the Sunningdale form is likely to be rejected by Unionists as representing a second victory for the SDLP in addition to the Irish dimension entrenched at Hillsborough. But besides power-sharing, there are many models of devolved government giving protection and influence to minorities: a number of them have been described in previous chapters. The discussion of various forms could well be high on the agenda of any tripartite meetings between the two Governments and the local politicians.

Until agreement on devolved government is reached, it is important that the momentum of the Hillsborough agreement is not lost. There are a number of reforms which are, in principle, welcomed by both sides. Both Catholics and Protestants have repeatedly called for a Bill of Rights; both Catholics and Protestants are worried about the use of accomplice evidence in courts; both Catholics and Protestants have now felt the impact of plastic bullets and have cause to welcome an improved system of civilian control of the police and an improved police complaints procedure. It should not be beyond human wit and patience to build some cautious progress on these foundations of shared concern. Progress in these areas could be made without prejudice, one way or the other, to the Hillsborough agreement. They are not matters, like the Flags and Emblems Act, where all the pressure for reform comes from a single side.

Any mainland citizen of the United Kingdom who studies the history of Northern Ireland must, at some point, ask himself: What are we doing there? Why should Northern Ireland remain part of the United Kingdom? Why should we, mainlanders, remain in the province and tax ourselves for its support?

Reasons for preserving the Union fall into three classes: reasons of self-interest, reasons of sentiment and reasons of morality. When Asquith's Home Rule Bill became law in 1914, reasons of all three classes strongly affected a large portion of the mainland British population. The strategic and economic interests of Great Britain were well served by the presence of a Loyalist and Unionist enclave in North-eastern Ireland. Many Englishmen, Scotsmen and Welshmen despised the Catholic Irish and felt a warm surge of affection for the sturdy Protestant settlers of the North. Moreover, even the Home Rulers had to admit that the moral arguments which made it wrong to subject Dublin to London rule by coercion made it wrong to subject Belfast to Dublin rule by coercion.

After Hillsborough, it is clear that the argument for retaining the

Union is now almost entirely a moral one. There is no longer any strategic or economic interest of the mainland to be served by retaining Northern Ireland separate from the Irish Republic. The average Englishman or Scotsman or Welshman feels no closer, in sentiment, to the Protestants of Northern Ireland than to the Irish Catholics, North or South: the greatest divide is rather between those who regard religion as important in politics (as do the great majority of Irishmen, North and South), and those whose politics are unaffected in general by religion (as are most of those who live on this side of the Irish Sea). The arguments of self-interest and sentiment have gone: and perhaps the saddest thing for the Unionists about Hillsborough was how clear it made the divergence of sentiment. There remains the moral argument. It is the clinching one. The Union must be preserved because, for the foreseeable future, the alternative to preserving it would be catastrophe for the inhabitants of the province, catastrophe for which we on the mainland could not escape a large share of the responsibility.

Index

137